L2

John Blakesley was born in 1950 and grew up in Chester. He studied theology in Oxford at Keble College and St Stephen's House. After spending twenty years as a parish priest in Cumbria, Yorkshire, and Co. Durham, he now lectures in liturgy at Durham University and is a Fellow and Tutor of St Chad's College. He is the Author of *Paths of the Heart* (SPCK) a volume of medieval prayers and poetry.

A Garland of Faith

For
Grace

'Gratia perficit nec tollit naturam' (St Thomas Aquinas)

A Garland of Faith

Medieval prayers and poems
newly translated and
arranged for the three year
Lectionary

by

John Blakesley

First published in 1998

Gracewing
2 Southern Avenue, Leominster
Herefordshire HR6 0QF

ISBN 0 85244 462 1

Typeset by Action Publishing Technology Ltd,
Gloucester GL1 1SP

Printed by Redwood Books
Trowbridge, Wiltshire BA14 8RN

Contents

PART I: THE SEASONS OF THE CHURCH'S YEAR

PART II: SAINTS' DAYS AND FESTIVALS

PART III: PASTORAL OCCASIONS

Introduction

'You never know when it might come in useful'

The human race can be roughly divided into two groups: there are hoarders, and there are chuckers. If you hear someone say 'It's time we had a good clear-out', you may be sure you are listening to a chucker. When chuckers are about to throw something away, hoarders reveal themselves as the people who say 'You never know when it might come in useful.'

I enjoy throwing away junk mail, but, with that single exception, I belong firmly and unashamedly in the hoarders' camp. Not only that, but I also cannot pass a rubbish-skip without having a look in it to see if it contains anything useful. Quite often it does, even if it's only a bit of wire. Even I must admit, however, that things do outlive their usefulness and must eventually be disposed of. Nevertheless, discarded objects will often contain parts which can be recycled and given a new lease of life. A car in a scrapyard may be horribly battered and completely undriveable, and yet still have components which can be salvaged. Fitted to another car, they can give several more years of useful service.

Rummaging in the scrapyard

This book is an exercise in recycling bits of discarded liturgy. Many of the pieces translated here are Sequences: poems which, beginning in the ninth century, used to be sung before the Gospel at Mass. Hymns at the Sunday Eucharist are a common feature of church life today, but in the Middle Ages the practice was unknown: hymns in those days were confined to the Choir Offices such as Lauds and Vespers. Sequences provided the only way in which people could give free expression to their devotion in contemporary language at the Church's central act of worship.

In the sixteenth century these popular poems were the victims of a massive clear-out. There had been about five thousand of them in use throughout Europe, but only four survived the Council of Trent. A fifth, the *Stabat Mater*, gained admittance to the Missal in 1727 and some continued to be used unofficially in France, but the liturgical chuckers had had a field day. In the nineteenth century, however, the

1

Victorian hoarding-instinct came into its own in the shape of scholars such as H. M. Bannister and J. M. Neale. Together with their continental colleagues they amassed large collections of Latin Sequence-texts taken from surviving medieval manuscripts and printed missals, and published them in scholarly editions. Rummaging through these works, one finds many pieces which probably deserved to be consigned to the scrap-heap. But one also finds gems which have been thrown out with the rubbish. Sometimes, too, a mediocre piece contains a passage whose thought, language, and imagery could well enrich the devotion of Christians in any age. It is these items which I have tried to rescue and polish up, for use in conjunction with the current versions of the Revised Common Lectionary.

Picking flowers

Buried at a deeper level than Sequences are the prayers from the ancient Gallican Rite, which I have taken from the *Missale Gothicum*. These date from the seventh century, and come from the eucharistic liturgy used in Gaul before the arrival of the Roman Rite in the eighth century. They are more effusive than the concise Roman prayers and would, if I had translated them in full, be very long-winded, but they often contain fresh and vivid poetic imagery.

Perhaps it is time to find a more fragrant analogy for the process of selecting these texts than that of poking about in a scrapyard. I shall settle for the one used by Benedict of Aniane, one of Charlemagne's liturgical advisers, who made a collection of Gallo-Roman prayers in the late eighth century to fill the gaps in the 'pure' Roman book sent by Pope Hadrian, thus making it usable in the churches of northern Europe. He described himself as 'plucking them like spring flowers from the fields, and gathering them together'. (*Praefatiuncula 'Hucusque'* in H. A. Wilson, ed., *The Gregorian Sacramentary*, Henry Bradshaw Society, 1915.) Since in a small way I have tried to follow in his footsteps, this book is called *A Garland of Faith*.

As well as the Sequences and the Gallican prayers, there are some non-liturgical poems, some prayers based on bishops' blessings, extracts from the notebook of a Saxon nun, and a variety of other material. Most of it is anonymous, but the book does contain the work of some reasonably well-known poets, for example: Notker, Gottschalk, Hildegard of Bingen, and Bernard of Cluny. As far as I know, none of the pieces has previously been translated into English, with the exception of four items from my *Paths of the Heart* (SPCK/Triangle 1993). After each translation is a comment relating it to the day's readings. Then, after the reference to the text's source, I have added a note on its background for those interested in the history of the liturgy.

There is an old monastic dictum which applies equally well to ordinary parish congregations: 'They pray best together who also pray alone.' Common worship and private prayer are both necessary for a healthy Christian life. This book is not intended to be an escape-route into a medieval fantasy-world. The authors of the texts translated here were real men and women trying to live their own lives of faith. I hope that entering into their thoughts and prayers will encourage us to meet the challenge of exercising an honest and authentic relationship with God in the midst of the realities of our lives today.

Poetry and prayer

What actually happens when we pray? There are plenty of books around which will tell you what their authors think ought to be happening, and many of these, I find, have the same sort of unsettling effect as medical text-books. You end up thinking there are all sorts of things wrong with you because you either recognize in yourself what seem to be symptoms of disease, or fail to recognize what are supposed to be symptoms of health.

In fact there are as many ways of praying as there are people who pray. One of the wisest maxims on prayer I have come across is: 'Pray as you can, not as you can't.' We are all different: God has created us as unique individuals and He wants us to be fully and gloriously ourselves, not pale imitations of St Teresa or St John of the Cross.

At a very simple level, there is, I suppose, a common thread which links our various experiences of praying. It is that, when we pray, there are thoughts about God somewhere in our minds. Since God indwells every atom of His Creation, He must surely be especially present in our thoughts about Him.

When we thank Him for particular blessings, or pray for other people, or express sorrow for our sins, we are bringing these aspects of our lives into the light of our consciousness, and placing them in the greater light of His presence.

But what happens when the focus shifts from our own concerns to what God is like in Himself? The wonder and beauty of the world and our longing for something deeper than its finitude can beckon us into a relationship with the Creator of the universe in which we live our lives, but our unaided reason cannot take us much further than that. For us truly to know Him and enjoy a relationship with Him, God must take the initiative and reveal Himself to us.

Christians believe that God has done just that in the person of Jesus. But getting to know another human being is not a simple matter. Our knowledge even of those closest to us remains partial and fragmentary. Literal descriptions of them cannot hope to encapsulate their essence: in order to begin to penetrate the mystery of their being, we need the resources of poetry. If human lovers constantly turn to poetic imagery to express the nature of their beloved ('My love is like a red, red rose'), how much more those who dare to think or speak or write of a Divine Love?

Our idea of who Jesus is, and therefore of what God is like, comes from the New Testament writings, especially the Gospels. Our access to the mind of Christ is primarily through the minds of the Evangelists. One of the virtues of this Lectionary is that, in devoting a year each to the Gospels of Matthew, Mark, and Luke, it gives us time to appreciate an Evangelist's particular flavour, and to see something of the distinctive light that each casts on the person of Jesus. Each in his own way uses poetic imagery to bring out the significance of the events he describes. The naked event of the Crucifixion consists of a rabbi dying a criminal's death on a Roman gallows. The New Testament writers clothe the event with interpretative imagery: it is the suffering of God's faithful servant; it is the sacrifice of the true Passover Lamb; the lifting-up of Jesus on the Cross is the exaltation of God's anointed King.

The poetic images of the Bible are not mere decorative fancy, dispensable at a pinch, like the icing on a cake: they are the very stuff of revelation, the means by which our minds lay hold on God.

The life-giving stream of Biblical imagery has flowed throughout the Church's history, constantly fed by the work of Christian writers and poets, and it goes on nourishing us today. In the Liturgy, verbal images are combined with visual ones and are embodied in sacramental acts. At the heart of every Eucharist, the rite which Jesus ordained to be his living memorial, are the great images of the Body and the Blood: the life broken and given and poured out for us in the form of bread and wine. Around these great images cluster a host of lesser ones, forming an ever-changing kaleidoscope of revelation. As the Church's Year goes round, the varying readings, prayers, and hymns produce new patterns of images, each reflecting in its own way an aspect of the mystery of God's love. Liturgy offers life-giving exposure to these images, and the work of poets is of its very essence. Their work can also enrich our relationship with God as we reflect on their writings in our personal devotions.

Claiming our inheritance

Bringing our own concerns into God's presence is an important part of prayer. So too is the more difficult business of making ourselves receptive to what God might want to 'say' to us. One way of doing this is to follow the recipe for appreciating beauty in nature or art, and the secret is to do nothing! We do not need to make an effort to enjoy beauty: we simply need to stop the wheels of our mind from turning, and allow ourselves time for the landscape or painting or music to make its impact upon us. So too with the truth and beauty of God as revealed through Scripture, liturgy, poetry, and prayer. In reading a Bible passage, prayer, or Christian poem, we need merely to give it our time and attention, so that its particular pattern of words and images may make its impression upon us. In doing this, we shall be growing in our knowledge of the true God revealed by Jesus: a God of endlessly creative and redemptive love, not the neurotic, life-denying tyrant of religious pathology.

Scripture and Tradition have bequeathed to us a rich inheritance of poetic images through which God extends to us His self-revelation in Jesus. Not all the items we have inherited will appeal to us: some will probably never suit our temperament, though they may be just the thing for someone else; some may come in useful at a later stage in our lives; and some may need to be adapted to our particular needs before we can use them and benefit from them. This book contains several examples of how Christians in the past have not been afraid to add to and adapt images which have come to them from Scripture and Tradition. In *The freedom of Grace*, set for Proper 4, Year B, the poet extends Isaiah's image of the clouds of heaven raining down the Just One (45.8) to include the idea of rain as a symbol of God's Grace which melts the winter of the old Law.

Making the best use of our inheritance could involve embellishing it with the aid of our own imagination. Notker did this in *Mary's offering*, set for 2 February. His imagination added to St Luke's story of the Presentation (2.22ff) the delightful detail of the smile on the child's face as he gazed up at Mary, in whose arms he was held. A tiny poetic brush-stroke has produced a vivid picture of the way God delights in us, as Mary did in her child, and of how we can rejoice that we are held securely in His love.

We too can imitate these poets' freedom in playing with Biblical images and using them in creative and distinctive ways. The rich diversity of our inheritance is there for us to explore, enjoy, and make our own.

'The train now standing ...'

Because lectionaries combine a system which is governed by the calendar date with one which depends on a variable Easter, books based on them cannot avoid the occasional quirky complexity, reminiscent of those in old-fashioned railway timetables. For example, rail travellers in mid-Wales in the 1950s needed to know that if the letter 'E' appeared beside a train in the timetable it meant 'Runs Saturdays only from Welshpool to Moat Lane Junction', whereas an 'X' signified 'Calls to set down at Talerddig on notice to Guard at Machynlleth.'

I have tried to avoid such footnotes in this book, but, because it aims to be as ecumenical as possible, provision has been made for those occasions when the Anglican and Roman Lectionaries deviate from their normally parallel tracks. When this happens, the translation which fits the Roman Lectionary is given (for purely alphabetical reasons!) after the one for Anglican use. Thus the Anglican 'Third Sunday of Epiphany' is the Roman 'Third Sunday in Ordinary Time'. In Years A and C the readings for this Sunday are more or less the same in both lectionaries and so the two titles appear together: 'Third Sunday of Epiphany – Third Sunday in Ordinary Time.' In Year B, however, the tracks divide and the readings are completely different. Consequently, the translation for the Roman 'Third Sunday in Ordinary Time, Year B' will be found after the Anglican 'Third Sunday of Epiphany, Year B', and the same principle applies throughout.

The book can also be used with the original version of the Revised Common Lectionary, pioneered in the United States and Canada, which follows the Roman line at those places (usually in the Epiphany Season) where it diverges from the Anglican one. Those who use this form of the RCL will still recognize the Kingdom Season, though it is not referred to as such, in the last four Sundays of the Church's Year, that is, the Thirty-First to Thirty-Third Sundays of Ordinary Time and the feast of Christ the King.

Perhaps those trains in mid-Wales now seem straightforward in comparison with the above, but I hope the complexities will prove tolerable for the sake of ecumenism.

I also hope that these recycled writings of medieval Christians will be found enjoyable and enriching by Christians today.

Ferryhill, Co. Durham
April 1998.

Sources of the
Translated Texts

After each translation and its commentary the opening words of the
Latin original are given, together with initials and a page-reference,
which indicate the source of the translated text. The initials refer to
these works:

AH: G. M. Dreves and C. Blume (eds.), *Analecta Hymnica Medii
Aevi*, Vol. 50 (Leipzig 1907).

BR: H. A. Wilson (ed.), *The Benedictional of Archbishop Robert*
(Henry Bradshaw Society 1903).

LS: J. Kehrein, *Lateinische Sequenzen des Mittelalters* (Mainz 1873,
reissued Hildesheim 1969).

MG: H. M. Bannister (ed.), *Missale Gothicum*, Vol. 1 (Henry
Bradshaw Society 1917).

NP: W. von den Steinen, *Notkeri Poetae Liber Ymnorum* (Bern
1960). This is a separate edition of the authentic Notker texts
taken from his two-volume work *Notker der Dichter und seine
geistige Welt* (Bern 1948).

OB: F. J. Raby (ed.), *The Oxford Book of Medieval Latin Verse*
(Oxford 1959).

PC: B. J. Muir (ed.), *A Pre-Conquest English Prayer-Book* (Henry
Bradshaw Society 1988).

RC: C. Hohler, 'The Durham Services in Honour of St. Cuthbert' in
C. F. Battiscombe (ed.), *The Relics of St. Cuthbert* (Oxford
1956).

SM: J. Wickham Legg (ed.), *The Sarum Missal* (Oxford 1916,
reissued 1969).

WP: D. Hiley, *Western Plainchant* (Oxford 1993).

YM: W. Henderson (ed.), *The York Missal*, Vol. 2 (Surtees Society
1872).

Sources of Information on Sequence-Repertories

In addition to the books containing the texts, I have relied on the following works to determine where and when the Sequences translated here were sung:

W. Arlt and G. Björkvall (eds.), *Recherches nouvelles sur les Tropes Liturgiques*, (Stockholm 1993).
This book contains three essays which give information about Sequence-repertories:
G. Iversen, 'Continuité et renouvellement à Nevers', pp. 276–81
(for the Augustinian house of St Martin, Nevers in the mid-twelfth century);
D. Hiley, 'Provins Bibliothèque Municipale 12 (24)', pp. 243–46 (for Chartres Cathedral in the thirteenth century); and
K. Schlager, 'Digna laude nunc melodya', pp. 416–7
(for the Cistercian house of Kaisheim-bei-Donauwörth about the year 1300).
M. Fassler, *Gothic Song* (Cambridge 1993), pp. 158f and 390ff
(for the four Parisian churches of Notre Dame, St Victor, Ste Geneviève, and St Denis in the twelfth and thirteenth centuries).
Dom Anselm Hughes OSB, *Anglo-French Sequelae* (Nashdom Abbey 1934, republished Farnborough 1966), pp. 18f and 129–35
(for a comparative table of English Uses. Hughes draws on all the early English Sequence-collections and some later missals, but does not include evidence from monastic *Ordinalia*).
A. Robertson, *The Service-Books of the Royal Abbey of St Denis* (Oxford 1991), pp. 176–84
(for St Denis, Paris in the thirteenth and fourteenth centuries).

Part I

The Seasons of the Church's Year

First Sunday of Advent

Come, Lord Jesus

> You govern all created things, O Lord,
> your royal sceptre in your strong right hand.
> Stir up your mighty power,
> and show it to your people.
> Grant them the gifts of your salvation,
> as your prophets promised from of old.
> From your shining kingdom in the heavens,
> come, Lord Jesus, come to this our earth.

This poem was probably written in the Kingdom of Aquitaine in south-western France early in the tenth century. When it was sung in church, it would have followed the singing of the verse from Psalm 80 'Stir up your strength, O Lord, and come to save us.' The poet develops this Advent theme in a way that expresses the longing of all God's creation for the coming of the promised Saviour, who will bring deliverance and freedom.

Qui regis, SM p. 461.

In the Middle Ages this Sequence was sung on the Third Sunday of Advent; to the first Sunday belonged the already well-known *Salus aeterna* ('Saviour eternal'), of which a version is in the *English Hymnal* and a modern translation in my *Paths of the Heart* (SPCK/Triangle 1993), p. 23.

Qui regis is found at Limoges and Winchester in the tenth century and (with the exception of Westminster Abbey, which had no Advent Sequences) was widely sung in England and France. The text has been translated in its entirety, which means that it is unusually short for a Sequence: in fact it is one of the few 'repetitionless' Sequences to have survived. The normal structure of an early Sequence consists of syllabically parallel double-versicles, because each phrase of the melody was sung twice, but in the case of *Qui regis* its melody was sung straight through without repetition.

Second Sunday of Advent

The herald's voice

He is the voice which goes before God's Word,
the friend who prepares for the bridegroom's coming,
and the morning star whose light brings in the dawn.

Once, hidden in his mother's womb, he greeted God's presence;
now he points openly to the Lamb of God.
He is the voice crying in the wilderness,
the herald of God's Word.

With burning faith and shining words he teaches many things,
and leads the multitudes to the true Light.
He himself is not that Light, but a lantern in the darkness
pointing to Christ, the eternal Light, who enlightens all the world.

The poet weaves together a number of biblical images and allusions as he presents to us his picture of John the Baptist, whose ministry combined fearless preaching of repentance with a self-effacing insistence that the One whom he proclaimed was greater than he. Isaiah's prophecy (40.3) of the voice crying in the wilderness, quoted in today's Gospel reading, is linked with John's own description of himself as the friend of the bridegroom: 'He must increase, but I must decrease' (John 3.29–30). The poet contrasts John's hidden greeting of Jesus when he leaped in Elizabeth's womb (Luke 1.41) with his open proclamation 'Behold the Lamb of God' in John 1.29.

    The prologue to St John's Gospel (1.8) describes the Baptist as a witness to the Light, not the Light itself, and later in that Gospel (5.35) Jesus calls John 'a burning and shining lamp'. The poet's imagination takes this imagery of light and develops it in a novel way: John is like the morning star whose shining heralds the greater light of the sunrise.

Vox praeit from *Ad honorem*, a Sequence for the feast of the Nativity of St John the Baptist, LS p. 253.

    The poet was almost certainly a twelfth-century Parisian, a canon either of Notre Dame or of the Augustinian abbey of St Victor. This abbey, founded in 1108, rapidly achieved a reputation as a centre of excellence for theology, spirituality, and Sequence-writing, associated respectively with the names of Hugh, Richard, and Adam.

As well as being in the repertoires of Notre Dame and St Victor, this Sequence was also sung in the royal abbey of St Denis, and is quoted by the sixteenth-century Parisian writer Clichtoveus. It does not seem to have been known in England.

Third Sunday of Advent

Pointing the way

John shows to us the path of truth and grace,
the way made ready for the Heavenly One;
we walk there safely if our hearts embrace
in humble faith and love God's own true Son.

For now God's bounty, free and unreserved,
allows the gates of heaven to be stormed
by force of love, and mercy undeserved
enriches hearts by penitence reformed.

This time of grace by prophets was foretold;
their words brief sparks which darkness did enmesh.
A greater prophet now is here: behold
his finger pointing to the Word-made-Flesh.

In Matthew 11.9 Jesus describes John the Baptist as 'more than a prophet': he is the messenger, promised by Isaiah, who prepares the way of the Lord. In verse 12 Jesus adds the puzzling saying that, since the time of John, violent men have been forcing their way into the kingdom of heaven. The text can be translated in various ways, but the interpretation placed upon it by this poet is that love is the force which gains entry to heaven's kingdom. John prepared the way for Christ's coming by preaching repentance, and Jesus continued this theme at the beginning of his ministry, saying 'Repent and believe the Gospel'.

Repentance (the original Greek word means 'a change of mind' or 'a change of heart') consists in accepting God's undeserved love and mercy, and placing our trust in that and not in ourselves.

Viam parat, stanzas 4b, 8, and 9 of the Sequence *Helisabeth Zachariae*, LS p. 258.

This Sequence in honour of St John the Baptist is found in a fourteenth-century Venetian manuscript. It was apparently unknown in France and England.

Fourth Sunday of Advent

Dew on the flower

The clouds of heaven distil their dew,
the streams flow down the mountain-sides,
the Root of Jesse sends up shoots.

From that root springs up a flower
which the prophet's foresight showed
in his mystic oracle.

Sprung from David's royal line,
Jesse's fruitful stem foreshows
Mary, maiden-mother blest,
and the flower her little child.

Brimming with the sevenfold grace
of the Holy Spirit's power,
God entrusts to us this flower:

by its beauty, scent, and savour
He delights us,
and invites us
to be made anew in Him.

The starting-point for this poet's meditation is this Sunday's Introit (Entrance Antiphon) from Isaiah 45.8: 'Distil your dew, O heavens, from above, and let the clouds rain down the Just One.' The dew and rain swell the mountain streams, which nourish the roots of the trees and produce new growth. Even barren-looking tree-stumps can sprout afresh if their roots can find water. So the Root of Jesse, King David's father (Isaiah 11.1), is an image of the barren womb of the Virgin, made fertile by the dew of God's Spirit, and bringing forth the flower which is Christ.

All the lovely things of God's creation, rain and dew, mountain streams and trees, are tokens of His love for us – gifts by which He seeks to delight us and help us to flourish; and the very essence of that love is distilled in the gift of His incarnate Son. He is the flower whose fragrance is diffused by the dew of the Holy Spirit. God's invitation to respond to His love is an invitation to find our deepest, truest selves, and to be created anew in Him.

Celi rorant from the Marian Sequence *Jubilemus Salvatori*, SM
p. 523.

Like *Ad honorem* (see p. 12) this is a twelfth-century product of the
school of St Victor in Paris. It found its way to England and occurs in
two of the three thirteenth-century manuscripts collated by J.
Wickham Legg in his edition of *The Sarum Missal* (Oxford 1916).
('Sarum Use' was the way services were ordered in Salisbury
Cathedral, but, as the Middle Ages went on, it became more and more
widespread in England and tended to displace other local Uses.)

The poem may be a Marian rewriting of another Victorine
Sequence beginning *Jubilemus Salvatori*, set for the Conversion of St
Paul. Such 'Marianizings' were common (perhaps the best-known
example being the Easter Sequence *Victimae Paschali laudes* which
became *Virgini Mariae laudes*) and were a result of the growing popularity of the Lady Mass. In the later Middle Ages nobles and rich
merchants were fond of endowing Lady Chapels in the larger
churches, often leaving enough money for a daily Sung Mass, hence
the need for large numbers of Marian Sequences.

This piece is an example of the Victorine poets' skill at blending
biblical images with symbols taken from the world of nature. It was
part of their balanced theology, Creation and Redemption being seen
as two aspects of the same loving, life-giving work of God. For more
on the Victorines see F. Raby, *A History of Christian-Latin Poetry*,
(Oxford 1953) pp. 355–75.

Christmas Eve

Earth and Heaven in harmony

The harmonies of heaven resound today on earth;
the angel-choirs on high sing of the virgin birth.

Shepherds, keeping careful vigil, hear the angel voices
singing songs of splendour, full of glory and of peace.

The things of earth are now made one with things above:
joy is ours, for God's own Word is joined to human flesh.

Bright stars announce his birth,
and starlight leads the shepherds into Bethlehem.
These men, who live by leading flocks of sheep,
find heaven's King among the animals.

He whose sovereign power extends through all that's made
lies here confined within a narrow manger.

Because the Incarnation of God's Son joins heaven and earth together, on this night human ears can hear the heavenly harmonies of the angels. In St Luke's story, which is tonight's Gospel reading, it is significant that the ears belong to shepherds, who were looked down on by the respectable not just because they were poor, but also because their outdoor way of life meant that they could not fulfil all the demands of the Law and so were religiously 'unclean'. How typical that the God whose Son was born in a cowshed should reveal that fact first to such people! The poet sees how appropriate it was that these men, who lived among their sheep, should find the Christ-child among the animals. The poem ends with another image of Divine humility: the God who fills the universe is confined by the hard wooden sides of a feeding-trough.

Celeste organum, a Christmas Sequence set in some Sarum manuscripts for the Mass of the Day and in others for the Mass of the Dawn, SM p. 462.

   The piece is first found in two Aquitanian manuscripts of the twelfth century but its style belongs to the tenth century. A measure of its popularity in England is the fact that one of its phrases, 'inter animalia', was used in a fifteenth-century carol, the 'Song of the Nuns of Chester' (*Qui creavit caelum* published in the *Oxford Book of*

Carols). The manuscript Processional from which it was taken dates from *c.* 1425. (The carol contains another line from an Incarnation Sequence: 'nascitur in stabulo' from *Missus Gabriel*, often sung at Lady Masses in Advent.)

To the medieval mind, inhabiting a pre-Copernican universe, musical harmony was itself an image of cosmic harmony. The early tenth-century musical theorist Regino of Prüm (following Cicero's *Dream of Scipio*) relates the music of the spheres to the eight notes of the diatonic scale sung or played by human musicians. In ascending order from the earth, the spheres (each with its governing planet or luminary) comprise: Moon, Mercury, Venus, Sun, Mars, Jupiter, and Saturn; each of these was thought to 'sing' a note of the scale from 'A' to 'G', and the Heavenly Sphere completed the octave with a top 'A'. (See M. Gerbert, *Scriptores ecclesiastici de musica sacra* (St Blasien 1784, republished Hildesheim 1990) Vol. I, p. 234.)

It was also believed that each sphere was presided over by an order of angels, with the ninth angelic order looking after the Earth. Early Sequence-texts are full of the idea that earthly voices in church blend with the celestial harmonies of angelic worship. A particular liturgical focus of this idea is the *Sanctus* chant in the Mass, when human voices sing the seraphic hymn 'Holy, holy, holy' from Isaiah 6. The alternate singing of Sequence verses by two sides of the choir could well be a conscious imitation of the seraphim who 'cried out one to another'. See Margot Fassler, *Gothic Song* (Cambridge 1993) p. 34, and Gunilla Iversen, 'Supera agalmata: angels and the celestial hierarchy in sequences and tropes' in E. Lillie and N. Petersen (eds.), *Liturgy and the Arts in the Middle Ages* (Copenhagen 1996) pp. 95–133.

Christmas Day

The light of Christ

From the starry city bright
down there came a golden light
which shone within a young girl's womb,
bringing blessings: captives freed,
healing for a world in need,
banishing earth's sin and gloom.

Bathing in its warm bright rays,
let all people join in praise
as the world's light has its birth.
Christ himself is this new light,
shining in our human sight,
life and health of all the earth.

The new light of Christmas morning points to the coming of the Light of the world, the light of God's love, which He has revealed to us in His Son. The light which enlightens all people shines in the dark places of the world, including the dark places of ourselves, and the darkness cannot overcome it (John 1.5). Through prayer and sacrament we can bathe in the light of God's love and experience in our own way some of the blessings of the light which the poet celebrates: the blessings of warmth, healing, and freedom. Perhaps this could mean the warmth of knowing that we are forgiven and accepted as we are, a warmth which allows old hurts to heal, and sets us free to accept and forgive others.

The two opening stanzas of *Ab arce syderea*, the first of the Marian Sequences in the Sarum Missal, SM p. 490.

This appears to be an English work dating from the late twelfth or early thirteenth century, and set to the melody of the Easter Sequence *Mane prima sabbati*. It is first found in MS Crawford lat. 24 in the John Rylands Library, Manchester, a Sarum book from Exeter dated between 1228 and 1256, which is Wickham Legg's 'Manuscript C' in his edition of SM.

According to Dom Anselm Hughes in *Anglo-French Sequelae* (Nashdom Abbey 1934, republished Farnborough 1966) the Sequence is an Advent one (p. 130), and, as well as being in the 'Crawford Missal', is found in manuscripts from Chichester, London, Lincoln, Norwich and St Andrews.

First Sunday of Christmas

Christ's childhood in the Holy Family

May God graciously teach and illuminate our hearts
with the spirit of His wisdom,
by which He wonderfully guided
the earthly childhood of His Son.

He willed that Christ should be subject to his human parents;
may He also fashion us according to His will
by His gifts of humility and holiness.

By His gift,
the child increased in grace and wisdom
as he advanced in years;
may He grant that our spirits too
may grow and flourish in His goodness.

We are forced to rely almost entirely on our imagination for a picture
of the life of the Holy Family. We know almost nothing of Christ's
hidden childhood years. The few glimpses given to us by the Gospel
writers do, however, show that the course of that family's life was not
always smooth. In St Matthew's story there is the flight into Egypt to
escape the murderous Herod, and in St Luke's Mary and Joseph experience the anguish of losing their child for three days – perhaps
foreshadowing the three days at the end of his earthly life when he
would be lost to sight and be supremely about his Father's business.
The author of this prayer sees that, in these bad times as well as in the
good ones, Christ's childhood was guided by God's wisdom. The
prayer asks for the gifts of humility and holiness, which will enable us
to accept whatever life offers us in the faith that God is always
working towards our true flourishing.

Deus qui filii, a bishop's blessing for the First Sunday after the
Epiphany, when the story of the Finding in the Temple was the Gospel
of the day, BR p. 7.
    The *Benedictional of Archbishop Robert* was probably written at
the 'New Minster' at Winchester in the second half of the tenth
century. It could have belonged either to the Robert who was
Archbishop of Canterbury until driven from his see in 1052, and who
died in Jumièges in 1070, or to the Robert who was Archbishop of
Rouen from 990 to 1037. The manuscript, though written in England,

passed into Normandy at some time before the middle of the eleventh century, where some more prayers were added to it.

For **Holy Family, Year B** see *Mary's offering* under 2 February in Part II.

Second Sunday of Christmas

God's love brings us back to Him

Let us recall in our devout praises
the joys that belong to this day,
in which that Light, most dear and welcome,
rises upon us.

The mists of night disperse,
our sin's shadows perish.
Joy is ours today, new health and salvation;
the Star of the Sea shines down upon the world.

Like a sheep which had been led astray,
fallen humanity is being called back to heavenly joys.
The Good Shepherd has come to seek out those who were
    perishing.

The celestial companies of angels are rejoicing today,
because the coin which was lost has been found.

God, who created all things, is born of a woman:
most blessed Child, in you our human nature is redeemed.

In today's Gospel St John unfolds the mystery of the Word-made-
flesh: God's Son, dwelling close to his Father's heart, reveals to us the
Divine nature, full of grace and truth. In celebrating the Incarnation,
this poet begins with St John's image of the Light shining upon the
world's darkness (John 1.5). As he explores what this image means,
he draws upon St Luke's parables of the lost sheep and the lost coin
(Luke 15.3–10). God's sending of His Son into the world shows that
He cares about us enough to come and find us, however lost we may
feel. He doesn't wait for us to reach Him; He comes to us where we
are.

Part of the Sequence *Eya recolamus*, SM p. 465.
    This Sequence was widely sung in England and Germany from the
eleventh century onwards. It occurs in fourteen English uses in places
as far apart as Exeter and Durham. In England it was usually sung on
the Feast of the Circumcision, whereas in the South German
Cistercian abbey of Kaisheim-bei-Donauwörth it was set for the
Christmas Dawn Mass.

It is very odd to find Cistercians singing Sequences at all: that austere Order generally regarded them as unnecessary and decadent elaborations of the liturgy which should be shunned. Kaisheim, however, had at least fifty-nine in its repertoire, and another Cistercian house, Hauterive in Switzerland, is known to have copied several manuscripts containing Sequences in its scriptorium. See Claire Maître, 'A propos de quelques tropes dans un manuscrit cistercien' in W. Arlt and G. Björkvall (eds.), *Recherches nouvelles sur les Tropes Liturgiques* (Stockholm 1993) p. 343, and Karlheinz Schlager, 'Digna laude nunc melodya', *ibid.*, p. 415.

(For the Epiphany, see 6 January in Part II.)

The Baptism of Christ

God's beloved Son

In the thirtieth year of his human life
God bent down beneath the hands of his renowned servant,
and so consecrated baptism to us for the forgiveness of our sins.

The Spirit, in the form of an innocent dove, came to him,
anointed him as foremost among all the holy ones,
and was happy to dwell for ever within his heart.

The Father's kindly voice resounded over the water;
forgotten were His former words:
'It grieves me that I made mankind';
now He says: 'Truly you are my Son,
most dear to me, in whom I am well-pleased.
Today, my Son, I have begotten you'.

This is part of a poem by NOTKER (*c.* 840–912), a monk of St Gall
in Switzerland. His portrayal of Christ's baptism is sensitive to the
echoes of the Old Testament in the Gospel accounts: the Spirit moving
over the face of the waters at the beginning of Creation (Genesis 1.2),
and the dove doing the same after the Flood (Genesis 8.8). Since New
Testament times Noah's Ark had been seen as a prefiguration of
baptism, being an image of salvation through water, and Notker
makes a striking contrast between God's angry voice at the time of the
Flood (Genesis 6.6–7) and His loving words to Jesus in the Jordan,
which echo Psalm 2.7 and Isaiah 42.1. The cumulative effect of these
echoes is to show that baptism (Jesus' and ours) is both New Creation
and Redemption, setting us free to live in the glorious liberty of the
children of God. Through our union with Christ in baptism, the
Father says to us too: 'You are my beloved child, in you is my delight'.

Anno hominis from *Festa Christi*, Notker's Sequence for the
Epiphany, NP p. 20.
   Notker, the 'little toothless stammerer' as he describes himself, was
a much-loved teacher at St Gall. He began writing his Sequences
during the decade of the 860s and he is the earliest known author of
them. He did not, however, invent the *genre*, as he tells us in the dedi-
catory letter (NP p. 6) with which he prefaced his Sequence-collection
in 884. He says that a priest from 'Gimedia' (probably Jumièges in
Normandy) had arrived at St Gall after fleeing from an attack by the

Vikings. He carried with him his antiphonary, in which verses had been set to the long melodies which followed the Alleluia-chant (*versus ad sequentias*). Notker approved of the idea, as he had always found the melodies difficult to remember, but, finding those particular examples not to his taste, he decided to try his own hand at writing words to Sequence-melodies. His first attempt was *Laudes Deo concinat* (NP p. 36); he showed this to his master Iso, who suggested that each note of the melody should correspond to just one syllable of text. Some scholars have concluded from this that Iso already knew the principles of Sequence-writing, but if so, one would expect him to have instructed Notker in the art, especially given his pupil's fallible memory! It is more likely that Iso, having seen Notker's first effort, decided that the one-note-per-syllable rule would make for a more effective mnemonic.

Notker went away and tried again, and produced *Psallat ecclesia*. This follows Iso's rule, and has the typically Notkerian verse-structure 'a, bb, cc,...h', thus combining elements of repetition and variation in a way which was to remain one of the Sequence's most aesthetically pleasing characteristics. A translation of it appears below in Part II under 'Dedication Festival'. For a discussion of the origins of the Sequence, see my article 'Creativity, Conservatism, and the Origins of the Sequence' in *Ushaw Library Bulletin and Liturgical Review*, No. 4, June 1997.

Festa Christi seems not to have been sung outside Germany.

Second Sunday of Epiphany – Second Sunday in Ordinary Time

Year A: see **Second Sunday of Advent**, 'The herald's voice', p. 12.

Year B: *Following God's way*

> Your divinity, O God, cannot be seen by human eyes;
> the vastness of Your being cannot be expressed in words.
> It is enough that we should simply love You as our Father,
> and revere Jesus as Lord;
> that we should receive You as our Creator,
> and embrace him as our Redeemer.
>
> Grant in Your mercy that we may climb up to You
> by that narrow way which You have shown us,
> and so reach our eternal happiness.
>
> Let us not be held back by any obstacles on our path,
> but let Your eternal salvation be all around us
> on the course of our journey.

Drawn by the disturbing but irresistible attractiveness of Jesus, the first disciples can have had little idea of just how risky a journey they were beginning when they responded to his call to follow him. It would cost them, in T. S. Eliot's words, 'nothing less than everything', but it was a way that led to life in all its fulness. For us too, following Christ's way will lead us, often through perplexing paths, to abundant life, to the discovery of who we really are. Christ is our Way and our Life, but he is also Truth: finding our true selves means being prepared to die to our many false selves, the masks of self-sufficiency with which we hide our insecurity, and which keep letting us down. The author of this prayer sees that Christ is not only the end of our journey, but his saving love is all around us on our way. We have only to put our hand into his to know that our ultimate security lies in him.

Cuius nec divinitas, part of the *Immolatio* or Proper Preface for the third Sunday Mass in the *Missale Gothicum*, MG p. 134.

The *Missale Gothicum* dates from the seventh century and is one of the few surviving examples of the ancient Gallican Rite, the way Mass was celebrated in what is now France before the Roman Rite gradually supplanted it during the eighth and ninth centuries.

The style of Gallican prayers tended to be wordy and repetitive, in contrast to the clear, concise, and carefully balanced phrasing of Roman prayers. Many of Cranmer's Collects in the Book of Common Prayer are superb translations of early Roman prayers which came into the Sarum Missal by way of Roman sacramentaries copied in Northern Europe. (A sacramentary is a book containing the priest's prayers; a missal also contains these, but with the addition of the readings and the choir-chants, which originally had been in separate books.)

Though often verbose, Gallican prayers did possess qualities usually lacking in Roman ones: a sense of drama (especially in the Holy Week Liturgy), emotional fervour, and a feeling for poetic imagery. Some of these Gallican elements enriched and enlivened the sober Roman Rite as it was celebrated in Northern Europe from the Carolingian period onwards. The Roman Rite in the later Middle Ages (of which the Sarum Use was an English 'dialect') amounted in fact to a Gallican-Roman synthesis, and some of its best-loved features – the drama of the Holy Week ceremonies, the poetry of the Sequences, and the tender devotion of the prayers before Communion – were fruits of the Gallican tradition of worship.

For a classic comparison of the Roman and Gallican Rites see Edmund Bishop's essay 'The Genius of the Roman Rite' in his *Liturgica Historica* (Oxford 1918).

Second Sunday of Epiphany – Second Sunday in Ordinary Time

Year C: *The Church's Bridegroom*

Rejoice, virgin Church,
as you celebrate again your spiritual marriage to Christ.
The kingly Wise Men share in the feast, bringing their symbolic
   gifts.
Here the bridegroom by his divine almightiness creates all things
   anew;
by his power he changes the water of Law into the wine of
   Gospel.

On this day he sanctifies the streams of the Jordan:
the Lord and King of heaven bends low to be a slave;
guiltless himself, he washes away your stains,
so that you may be clean and holy for him,

worthy to share his bed and his royal crown;
a mother of children, yet a pure virgin;
and be fit to live with him in the palace of heaven,
enjoying the glory of the angels, which gladdens the heart.

Thither may he bring us all, who serve him.

More than once in his parables Jesus used the image of a marriage-feast to convey the joyful and celebratory character of life lived within the Kingdom (or Reign) of God. The prophets, especially Hosea, had portrayed God's relationship with His often faithless people in terms of a marriage, and, following Ephesians, Christian poets applied this wedding-imagery to the love between Christ and his Church. This poet links the three Epiphanytide stories of the Wise Men, Jesus' baptism, and the Cana miracle, and makes present-giving, washing, and celebration into elements of the spiritual marriage-feast to which Christ invites us. The sign at Cana 'on the third day' points to the Risen Christ as our loving bridegroom who is creating us anew, and whose presence can transform the water of duty into the wine of delight.

Gaude virgo ecclesia, YM p. 318.
   This is one of two Sequences which were added to the first folio of the Oxford manuscript (Bodley 775) of the Winchester Troper, a

collection of Tropes and Sequences written at Winchester (then the capital of the Saxon kingdom of Wessex) about the year 1000. The additions were probably made at some time in the eleventh century.

This Sequence was sung at Epiphanytide at Hereford as well as at Winchester.

Third Sunday of Epiphany – Third Sunday in Ordinary Time

Year A: *Light of the world*

> Light has arisen, and has shone on the people
> who sat in the dark shadow of death;
> the poor of the world can rejoice,
> because a little child has been born of a virgin.
>
> So that sinful humanity might rise up to heaven,
> the God-Man came down to share our human poverty.
> We praise God and are glad
> as we gaze in wonder at this new work of grace.
>
> How full of joy is this hidden mystery!
> How worthy of our praise is this marvel of God's gracious
>   humility!
> Human minds cannot penetrate its secret,
> nor can subtle arguments untie its knot.
>
> Our reason cannot grasp God's mighty works,
> but we can truly know Him, for in Christ
> the Father has revealed to us Himself.

St Matthew sees the life of Jesus as fulfilling Isaiah's oracle about Galilee: 'The people who walked in darkness have seen a great Light' (9.2). The light of God's love shines upon our darkness, and God Himself shares human poverty. Jesus overturns conventional religion, which saw the poor as lacking God's blessing: he assures them that they are heirs to all the riches of God's Kingdom. This poet also sees that we cannot explore the mystery of God by the light of human reason, but, as Peter discovered at Caesarea Philippi and at the Transfiguration, the light that shines in the face of Christ is the revelation of the glory of the living God.

Lux est orta, a Christmas Sequence found in a missal printed in 1520 for the Franciscans of Paris, LS p. 33.

The simplicity of their Order meant that the use of Sequences was not encouraged among the Franciscans, though they were not as firmly opposed to them as were the Cistercians and Carthusians. In view of this, it is ironic that two of the greatest Sequences ever written, the *Stabat mater* and the *Dies irae*, should have come from a

Franciscan milieu! As well as the principle of simplicity, there was a practical reason for the fact that Franciscan service-books tended to be 'slim-line': the nature of the friars' ministry meant that they were often on the move and so needed easily portable liturgical books. Similarly, the highly mobile officials of the Papal Curia also needed lightweight books to take on their administrative journeys, hence the adoption at Rome of the Franciscan version of the liturgy in the later thirteenth century. Between 1277 and 1280 Pope Nicholas III actually ordered all non-Franciscan liturgical books to be burned!

Most Franciscan chant-books had between 8 and 10 Sequences in an appendix, but the Franciscans of Paris were an exception to the rule. Since the time of Adam of St Victor (see p. 12) Paris had been the major European centre for the composition of Sequences, as it was for polyphony. In 1256 the Parisian friars received Papal permission to use more Sequences in Masses of the Holy Spirit and of Our Lady, and their repertoire grew to over 70. The 1520 Missal from which this poem comes contains no fewer than 162! (See LS p. 21, and S. Van Dijk and J. H. Walker, *The Origins of the Modern Roman Liturgy*, (London 1960) pp. 395ff.)

It is tempting to suppose that the author of *Lux est orta* was himself a Parisian Franciscan: he is clearly well acquainted with the 'subtle arguments' of the University 'schoolmen', and he has a typically Franciscan concern for the poor.

Third Sunday of Epiphany

Year B: see **Second Sunday of Epiphany, Year C,**
The Church's Bridegroom, p. 28.

Third Sunday in Ordinary Time

Year B: see **Third Sunday of Advent,** *Pointing the way*, p. 14.

Third Sunday of Epiphany – Third Sunday in Ordinary Time

Year C: see **Christmas Day,** *The Light of Christ*, p. 19.

Fourth Sunday of Epiphany

Year A: see **Second Sunday of Epiphany, Year C,**
The Church's Bridegroom, p. 28.

Fourth Sunday in Ordinary Time

Year A: as below for **Year B,** *Christ our teacher,* p. 32.

Fourth Sunday of Epiphany – Fourth Sunday in Ordinary Time

Year B: *Christ our teacher*

> The Lord Almighty
> has graciously allowed us to hear his word;
> may he grant us knowledge
> of the great mysteries of his kingdom.
>
> May he fill our minds with the plentiful seed of his Word,
> and be pleased with its fertile growth within us.
>
> May he defend us against all temptation,
> and, as the riches of his grace multiply within us,
> may we bring forth fruit,
> thirty, sixty, and an hundredfold.

Jesus taught with authority because he was not passing on truths learned at second hand, but was speaking from the depths of his own personal experience and knowledge of the Father. A recurring theme of his teaching is the unstoppable exuberance of growth in the world of nature. This of course was a fact of life for his hearers as it is for us. We can see growth happening in the unlikeliest and most hostile environments: rowan trees clinging to bare rock crevices on mountain-sides, or birch trees colonizing the stony ballast on railway lines. This, says Jesus, is what the Kingdom of God is like: His loving purposes are exuberant, ingenious, and ultimately unstoppable. Frustrated in one direction, they will find a way of getting there in the end.

He does of course invite us to co-operate with His purposes. When His teaching has planted the seed of His Word in our hearts, we can help to nourish its growth by being faithful in our Christian living. But we can only do so much: there will be times when we must simply wait patiently and trustingly for God's loving and life-giving work to bear its fruit.

Det vobis, the Blessing for Sexagesima Sunday, when the Gospel of the day was the Parable of the Sower, BR p. 9.

Fourth Sunday of Epiphany

Year C: see '2 February', *Mary's offering*, p. 151.

Fourth Sunday in Ordinary Time

Year C: see 'Proper 9, Year B', *The Spirit's Inbreathing*, p. 110.

Fifth Sunday before Lent – Fifth Sunday in Ordinary Time

(**Fifth Sunday of Epiphany**, Sunday between 3 and 9 February)

Year A: *A light in the darkness*

On the fourth day of Creation, by a power too wonderful for
   words,
God ordained that the glorious splendour of the sun,
the pale radiance of the moon,
and the shining courses of the stars
should move amid the clouds of the sky;
may the light of His blessing shine into the depths of our hearts.

He is the source of light,
and the eternal splendour of all the saints;
may He set our inmost being on fire with His love,
and enlighten us with His wisdom;
may we be aglow with graces like the stars of heaven.

When we come to lay down the burden of our flesh,
may He admit us to the fellowship of heaven's citizens,
so that we may share in the eternal glory of the saints,
and wear the crown of everlasting joy.

Today's Gospel reminds us of our vocation, as individuals and as a
Church, to shine like a light in an often dark world. But, like the
moon, we can only give out light if we first receive it from our Sun.
We must give ourselves time to bathe in the warm radiance of God's
love for us, and absorb it into the depths of our being, if we are to
show that love to others.

Benedicat et inluminet, the weekday Blessing for Wednesdays, BR
p. 49.
    In the medieval Benedictionals the blessings for weekdays reflected
the work of God in the first week of Creation in Genesis 1.
Wednesday was the fourth weekday (*Feria quarta*) and so the theme
was God's creation of the great lights of heaven on the fourth day.
The same creation-centred themes run through the weekday Office
Hymns for Vespers (see *English Hymnal* numbers 58 to 62). The
hymn which corresponds to this prayer is number 60, with its verse:

Who, on the fourth day, didst reveal
The sun's enkindled flaming wheel,
Didst set the moon her ordered ways,
And stars their ever-winding maze.

Fifth Sunday before Lent – Fifth Sunday in Ordinary Time

(Fifth Sunday of Epiphany, Sunday between 3 and 9 February)

Year B: *Signs of Godhead*

> Let us praise our Saviour in humility,
> and devoutly rejoice in our heavenly Lord, the Messiah.
> To save lost humanity, to bring us our liberty,
> he emptied himself, hiding in human flesh the glory of his
>   Godhead.
>
> He suffered hunger, he knew weariness and sadness,
> and yet in his humble bodily life his divinity was revealed,
> showing itself in his teachings and signs.
>
> Blind eyes he clothed with bright and shining light;
> lurid leprosy was banished by his calm and healing touch.
> Tongues that were dumb or halting he released;
> he opened ears long deaf to human speech.
>
> He walked upon the lake's rough waves as though
> on firm dry land; he stilled the stormy winds.
> He drove out fevered madness, cured weak limbs;
> from their decay he raised the dead to life.

NOTKER (see pp. 24–25) was a theologian as well as a poet. Despite using the metaphor of Jesus' divinity being 'hidden' in human flesh, he makes it very clear that Christ's humanity was no mere cloak or disguise, but was absolutely real. For Notker, God in Christ shows His solidarity with human beings by sharing our limitations, our weakness, and our pain. The signs of Christ's divinity are not magic tricks; they are all of a piece with his teaching and they demonstrate his absolute commitment to human flourishing. He therefore acts to overcome everything which threatens that abundant life: the raging of the elements, the raging of a disturbed psyche, the diseases which diminish human lives. All these point to the great healing miracle: his victory over Death.

Selected verses from *Laudes salvatori*, Notker's Sequence for Easter Day, NP p. 26.

England's close relationship with France, especially of course after the Norman Conquest, meant that the two countries shared a great many Sequences in common. While it is rare to find German Sequences being sung in France, several of them became very popular in England, and one of these was *Laudes salvatori*. It is found in the tenth-century Winchester sources, and at Sarum it was the Sequence for Low Sunday.

It may in fact provide a possible answer to the puzzle of how Low Sunday got its name. In France that Sunday is called *La Quasimodo* from the first word of the Introit 'Like new-born babes ...'. Could it be that in England it was called 'Laudes Sunday' after its well-known Sequence? 'Low Sunday' pronounced with a northern accent sounds very like 'Laudes Sunday'.

Admittedly, it was not sung everywhere on that Sunday: in York the Canons of the Minster sang it on Easter Monday, but the Benedictines of St Mary's Abbey followed the custom of the Sarumite majority and sang it on Low Sunday.

Fifth Sunday before Lent – Fifth Sunday in Ordinary Time

(Fifth Sunday of Epiphany, Sunday between 3 and 9 February)

Year C: *The call of the first disciples*

Eternal God, You turned blessed Peter away from his earthly
   skills at fishing,
and called him to the practice of heavenly wisdom,
so that he might set the human race free from the depths of this
   world
by means of the net of Your teachings.

Blessed John received his calling from our Lord Jesus Christ Your
   Son;
he left his earthly father so that he might find a heavenly one;
he threw away the nets of this world, which had enmeshed him,
so that with a free mind he might seek the gifts of eternity.

He left his boat bobbing on the waves,
in order to steer the Church on a calm and peaceful course.
He turned from probing the depths of the sea
to gazing into the mysteries of God.

In today's Gospel Jesus says to Simon Peter 'Do not be afraid; from
now on it is men you will catch' (Luke 5.10). This seventh-century
writer goes on to develop the contrasts and continuities between the
former lives of these Galilean fishermen and their later work as apostles. Instead of seeing a fishing-net as something which confines and
constricts, he treats it as the means by which Peter 'liberated' fish
from the depths of the sea! It thus becomes an image of his preaching
the Gospel which sets men and women free. John's nets, however, are
treated more conventionally: they represent the worldly cares which
enmeshed him before he left them behind to seek the things of heaven.
But there is still continuity between his old life and his new one: he
still gazes into the depths, not of the sea, but of the mystery of God.
As St Thomas Aquinas said, 'Grace perfects nature, it does not take it
away'; the working of God's grace in our lives does not obliterate our
natural inclinations and skills, but enhances them to His glory.

Part of the *Immolatio* (Preface) *Praecipue hodie* for the feast of SS
Peter and Paul, and of *Beati Johannis* for the feast of St John the

Evangelist in the *Missale Gothicum* (see p. 26), MG pp. 94 and 107.

In seventh-century Gaul St John was commemorated on 6 May, the day which was kept in the later Western Church as St John before the Latin Gate. The Gallican Church observed 27 December as the feast of both the brothers James and John, which was the custom in the East.

Fourth Sunday before Lent – Sixth Sunday in Ordinary Time

(**Sixth Sunday of Epiphany,** Sunday between 10 and 16 February)

Year A: *A prayer for God's Grace*

> The Holy Spirit's grace be with us all:
> may He drive out all evil from our souls,
> and make our hearts a dwelling for Himself.
>
> O loving Spirit, light of humankind,
> dispel the inner darkness of our fear.
>
> O Holy One, You always look with love
> upon the thoughts and feelings of our hearts:
> pour out Your tender balm upon our souls,
> anoint our senses with Your gentle grace.
>
> You cleanse us from the things which cause us shame;
> keep pure and clear our spirits' inward sight,
> that we may know the Almighty Father's will,
> and seek His face in purity of heart.

Experience teaches us that we are unable in our own strength to fulfil Christ's new law of love. We are often so sunk in our own concerns that we fail to notice what God may be asking of us. We need the help of the Holy Spirit's grace firstly to clarify our vision so that we are alert and ready to do God's will, and then we need His encouragement and strength to put love into practice, thus finding – through generosity – true riches and lasting treasure. In this poem NOTKER sees that the root cause of our failure to love is fear: perfect fear casts out love just as surely as perfect love casts out fear. He pictures fear as darkness: the light of God's love dispels the darkness, restoring our courage and confidence. The more we realize that we are always surrounded by that light and warmly enclosed in that love, the more we can generously show love to others.

Sancti Spiritus assit, Notker's Sequence for Pentecost, NP p. 52 (text); p. 90 (text and melody).

 This is one of the few pieces to cross the frontier dividing the French and German Sequence-repertoires. It was sung all over Europe at Pentecost, usually on the feast itself, but in a few places, for example at Nevers, it was assigned to one of the days in the Octave.

Fourth Sunday before Lent – Sixth Sunday in Ordinary Time

(Sixth Sunday of Epiphany, Sunday between 10 and 16 February)

Year B: *Christ our Healer*

May Almighty God heal all the scars of our sins,
as Christ, by his own touch,
lovingly cleansed the leper who asked for healing.

He was willing to visit and heal the centurion's servant;
may he enter into our hearts with his love and mercy,
and make them his dwelling-place.

By his guidance,
may we grow into fullness of faith and trust in him,
so that we may enjoy the rest and refreshment of the kingdom
    of heaven
in the company of his saints.

God's passionate desire for human wholeness was incarnated in Jesus' ministry of healing. According to some manuscripts of Mark 1.41 Jesus was angry at the leper's suggestion that he might not want to heal him. 'Of course I want to', says Jesus. In reaching out and touching the leper, Jesus showed God's love for those whom society puts beyond the pale. The action was a costly one, not just in terms of the risk of physical contagion, but also because it put Jesus outside the law of religious purity.

His willingness to visit the house of the Gentile centurion (Luke 7.1–10) was also morally defiling, but, here as always, Jesus considered showing God's love for the outcast to be more important than ritual purity. He is not interested in our piety or respectability; he comes to us as we are, in our flawed and imperfect humanity, and brings to the wounds of our inner selves his healing touch.

Omnipotens Deus, the Blessing for the Third Sunday after the Epiphany in the *Benedictional of Archbishop Robert* (see p. 20), BR p. 8.

On this Sunday the Gospel of the day was the Matthaean account of the leper and the centurion's servant in 8.1–13.

Fourth Sunday before Lent – Sixth Sunday in Ordinary Time

(**Sixth Sunday of Epiphany,** Sunday between 10 and 16 February)

Year C: *The fountain of life*

> As the thirsty deer longs for the welcome waters,
> so the faithful soul hastens towards God, the fountain of life.
>
> As the banks of a running stream afford refreshment,
> so the mind, thirsting for truth, finds its satisfaction in God.
>
> What good things You shower upon Your servants, O Lord!
> How they deprive themselves, those who depart from You, the
>   eternal light!
>
> Those who desert You reap to themselves labour and sorrow,
> but whoever seeks You finds gladness and peace.

The poor and needy are called happy by Jesus, because they are unlikely to make the mistake of trusting to themselves or their possessions for their ultimate security. Those who do make that mistake are compared by Jeremiah (17.5–8) to a bush growing in a dry wasteland. It may seem to flourish for a time, but, when drought comes, its roots cannot find water and it withers. He contrasts the self-reliant with those who look to God for their ultimate security: they are like the tree planted by the water-side; even when the surface of their lives is dry and arid, they have their roots in God and draw their nourishment from the fountain of life itself.

In this poem BERNARD OF CLUNY expresses our need of God and our longing for Him by means of the image of the thirsty deer in Psalm 42.1: 'As a hart longs for flowing streams, so longs my soul for thee, O God.' In drought and in plenty, the constant stream of God's love revives and refreshes us. 'Come to me', says Jesus, 'all who labour and are heavy laden ... and you will find rest for your souls' (Matthew 11.28–29).

Ut iucundas, the beginning of a long poem, the *Mariale*, in honour of the Blessed Virgin Mary, OB p. 226.

This Bernard (*c.* 1140) is sometimes called 'of Morlas', from his birthplace in the Pyrenees (often confused with Morlaix in Brittany). He was a monk of Cluny in the time of the famous abbot Peter the

Venerable. His most famous work is an extended poem called *De contemptu mundi*, also known from its opening line as *Hora novissima*. Its general air of pessimism is relieved by some visionary passages about the heavenly Jerusalem; a translation of one of these is the hymn 'Jerusalem the golden'.

Third Sunday before Lent – Seventh Sunday in Ordinary Time

(**7th Sunday of Epiphany**, Sunday between 17 and 23 February if earlier than 2nd Sunday before Lent)

Year A: *Christ our life*

> Let us ask Almighty God that he would always watch over us,
> and keep us devoted to Him in eager service,
> happy to be members of His family and household.
>
> For the sake of our redemption
> he took on the fragile substance of this earth.
> He came to us in a human body;
> he taught us by the words of his preaching,
> and by sharing with us the life which he lived in our midst.
> He embraced our mortality,
> and redeemed us by tasting death on our behalf.
>
> He has made us rich
> by pouring upon us the spirit of his divine life.
> With the Father and the Holy Spirit he lives and reigns,
> God for ever and ever.

Our minds cannot grasp the immensity of God's being, but in Christ God shares with us His divine life and deals humanly with His human creatures. God puts Himself in our midst in the person of Jesus; his words and actions, his suffering and dying reveal the depth of God's love for us. Jesus embodies the love of God in all its lavish and costly generosity, and, through the gift of the Spirit, the riches of the divine life are poured upon us.

The more we realize how rich we are in being thus loved by God, the more we are able to respond with an answering generosity in our dealings with others, including those who hurt us. We are enabled to see that in welcoming others we are welcoming Christ; his humility teaches us the paradox that humble acts of service help us to discover our own true freedom.

Omnipotentem Deum, a Christmas *Praefatio* from the *Missale Gothicum* (see p. 26) MG p. 4.

In the Gallican Rite the *Praefatio* was a prayer of admonition addressed to the people, encouraging them to pray earnestly to God.

It followed the Offertory Procession when the bread and wine were brought to the altar. Like most of the prayers in the Gallican Mass, it varied according to the season of the Church's Year. See W. S. Porter, *The Gallican Rite* (London 1958), pp. 31ff.

Third Sunday before Lent – Seventh Sunday in Ordinary Time

(**7th Sunday of Epiphany**, Sunday between 17 and 23 February if earlier than 2nd Sunday before Lent)

Year B: *The life-giving Trinity*

> O God, Almighty Father, Creator of all things,
> Source and Fountain of goodness, Light eternal;
> save us by Your kindness, loving Lord,
> and have mercy upon us.
>
> O Christ, splendour of God, power and wisdom of the Father,
> you shape and form our humanity, and restore us when we fall;
> let not your creatures be lost, kind Jesus,
> but have mercy upon us.
>
> O Holy Spirit, proceeding from them both, and the bond of
>   their love,
> fountain of life, fuel of love's fire, strength that makes us holy,
> cleanser of guilt, giver of abundant pardon;
> cancel our sins, fill us with the sacred gift of Yourself,
> O nourishing Spirit, and have mercy upon us.

The context of our life in Christ is the mystery of the Trinity, that eternal society of love which existed before all worlds and is without end. 'Infinite love is the link/tying the trio above' wrote St John of the Cross in one of his poems (ed. J. F. Nims, New York 1968, p. 49). The Holy Spirit, the bond of love between Father and Son, is poured into our hearts, making us God's sons and daughters. As his children we are promised the best of His good gifts: grace (bringing forgiveness), and resurrection. These gifts of the loving and life-giving Trinity are shown in the story of the paralytic (Mark 2.1–12). His body is carried by four men, lowered through a hole, and lies at the feet of Jesus, where, as a child of God, he is told: 'Arise, your sins are forgiven.' Our true security and value lie in our status as God's children, not in what we own (Luke 12.15). The Canaanite woman found that there are no limits to God's merciful love (Matthew 13.21), and Peter learned that God's endless generosity to us is to be reflected in our willingness to forgive others (18.21).

Cunctipotens genitor, a Trope to the *Kyrie*, YM p. 244.

Tropes, like Sequences, first appeared in the ninth century, that period of extraordinary creativity which saw a flourishing of the visual arts, the birth of modern drama and musical polyphony, and a great outpouring of liturgical poetry. By the early years of the century Charlemagne's policy of Christian education through the monastic and cathedral schools had borne fruit: there was a new generation of poets eager to embellish the Church's liturgy with their work. Opportunities for this were limited because the words and music of the Mass were fixed by authority, but, here and there, gaps in this liturgical ring-fence were found through which the work of the new poets could be smuggled. These gaps were the places where the chants contained *melismata*, successions of notes sung to the same syllable of text. In place of the extended vowels of the original text, choirs in some churches began to sing the newly-composed words of the poets.

The longest *melismata* were those sung to the final 'a' of the Alleluia before the Gospel, and this was the context of the earliest Sequences (see p. 25), the length of the melodies being reflected in the length of the Sequence-texts. Shorter *melismata* were to be found in the other Mass-chants, both the fixed ones of the 'Ordinary' (*Kyrie*, *Gloria*, *Sanctus* and *Agnus Dei*) and the variable ones of the 'Proper', now often replaced by hymns (Introit, Gradual, Offertory, and Communion). The words set to these shorter *melismata* are known as Tropes; this one, *Cunctipotens genitor*, was sung to the extended 'e' of *Kyrie* and *Christe* in the chant *Kyrie eleison* ('Lord, have mercy'). Dating from the late tenth or early eleventh century, it was popular all over Europe.

Tropes and Sequences were not without their critics in the ninth century: there was a school of thought, championed by Bishop Agobard of Lyons and the deacon Florus, which disapproved of anything non-Biblical being sung in church, and the bishops at the Council of Meaux in 845 ordered deposition for any cleric who sang these new chants. Despite the threats the two *genres* flourished: only after the twelfth century did the popularity of Tropes begin to wane, and Sequences, having adopted rhythm and rhyme, survive to this day.

Third Sunday before Lent – Seventh Sunday in Ordinary Time

(7th Sunday of Epiphany, Sunday between 17 and 23 February if earlier than 2nd Sunday before Lent)

Year C: *Christ our life*, p. 44.

Second Sunday before Lent (Creation Sunday)

Joy in Creation

Let us all rejoice in our God, who created all things
and set the universe on its foundations:
the sky, sparkling with the varied light of a myriad stars;
the shining splendour of the sun, giving order to the world;
the moon, adorning the night with her beauty;
sea and land, mountains, plains, and deep rivers;
the vast open spaces of the air,
through which the birds and the winds fly, and the rains fall.
All these things combine to serve You alone, O God our Father;
now and through all the ages of eternity their praise resounds
    to Your glory.

For our salvation You sent Your only Son to this earth;
guiltless himself, he suffered for our sins.
O Trinity, we ask You to rule over our hearts and bodies,
and grant to us sinners Your pardon and protection.

In one of her visions, the fourteenth-century anchoress Julian of Norwich saw the whole of God's Creation as a little round thing, the size of a hazelnut, on the palm of her hand. She saw that everything owes its existence to the love of God, that it is made, loved, and sustained by Him, and that He is everything that is good (*Revelations of Divine Love*, ed. C. Wolters, Harmondsworth 1966, p. 68). In his own way, the author of this text, a French poet writing about four hundred years before Julian, also invites us to rejoice in the beauty, variety, and goodness of Creation, for God Himself 'saw everything that He had made, and behold, it was very good' (Genesis 1.31).

Jubilemus omnes, YM Vol. 1, p. 11.

This Sequence was sung throughout England and France on the Fourth Sunday of Advent. It is found in the earliest of the Limoges tropers (Paris B. N. lat. 1240), dated between 933 and 936, but it probably originates in the ninth century. Its melody was known as *Veni Domine*, from the Alleluia-verse for Advent IV 'Come, Lord, and do not delay'; Sequences for feasts of Virgins were also written to its melody, hence its alternative title *Adducentur*, an allusion to the verse from Psalm 45 'The virgins that be her fellows shall be brought unto the King'. Notker used the same melody for his Sequence *Stirpe Maria regia*, for the feast of Our Lady's Nativity.

This lovely tune is printed by Dom Anselm Hughes (see p. 19) and discussed in detail on his pp. 76ff. He cites no fewer than 202 manuscripts containing the melody; 55 of these have the text of *Jubilemus omnes*. There is a more recent discussion in R. L. Crocker, *The Early Medieval Sequence* (Berkeley 1977) p. 341.

A rubric preceding this Sequence in a manuscript York Missal gives an interesting glimpse of how this piece would have been performed in the Minster in the fourteenth century. The words are to be sung by four Vicars Choral in black copes standing in the pulpit, while the choir repeats the melody, singing the vowel 'a', after each verse except the last. This manuscript (Henderson's MS. C in his edition of YM) had been given to the parish church of Cuckney in Nottinghamshire, but its rubrics indicate that either it had been written for use in the Minster or it had been copied from a Cathedral book. In terms of Sequence-performance, the situation it describes seems to be an English *via media* between the contrasting methods used in France and Germany. Firm evidence is hard to come by, but the fact that most lines in a French Sequence end in an 'a'-vowel suggests a simultaneous performance, with cantors singing the words while the choir sang the melody to the final vowel of 'Alleluia'. German Sequences appear to have been sung antiphonally, with each verse divided between the two halves of the choir. The York method is French in its retention of the 'a'-vowel, but German in that nothing obscures the singing of the words.

Eighth Sunday in Ordinary Time

Year A: see Second Sunday of Epiphany, Year B, *Following God's Way*, **p. 26.**

Year B: *The spiritual marriage*

> Rejoice, O virgin mother Church!
> Now you are pledged to Christ
> in the bonds of marriage,
> with an eternal dowry,
> with a robe of beauty,
> and an immortal glory.
>
> The human soul as bride is joined to Christ:
> Christ and the Church, no longer two, but one.
>
> She is to reign with him in heaven's glory,
> tasting eternal joy through all the ages,
> when God shall be all in all.

Jesus compares himself to a bridegroom, and the Kingdom of Heaven to a wedding-feast. The old relationship with God, enshrined in commandments and rules, has been swept away; the new, loving, and intimate relationship which Jesus brings is as fresh, sweet, and joyful as new wine at a marriage-banquet. This eleventh-century poet takes the image of the Church as Christ's Bride and develops it in a way that reveals its consequences for the individual Christian. Christ the Bridegroom incarnates God's love for the whole community of His people, but each of us as a member of that community is delighted in by God with an unique and special love.

Selected verses from *Gaude virgo mater*, YM p. 317.

This, together with *Gaude virgo ecclesia*, was one of the two eleventh-century Sequences added to the Oxford manuscript of the Winchester Troper (see p. 28). It was set at Winchester and St Albans (*c.* 1140) both for the Epiphany and the Feast of the Dedication of a Church.

Eighth Sunday in Ordinary Time

Year C: *A prayer for fruitfulness*

Do not ever abandon, O Lord, the vine which You have planted,
but graciously tend it and cultivate it always.

Do not let it be choked by brambles
nor despoiled by the raids of greedy birds,
but stand by it always,
so that each day it may bring forth abundant clusters of grapes.

Do not let the enemy sow tares in Your vineyard,
but let it ever bear fruit which is worthy of You.

We ask this through Christ our Lord,
who lives and reigns with You and the Holy Spirit,
God for ever and ever.

The prophets and psalms compared the people of Israel to a vine
(Psalm 80.8ff) or a vineyard (Isaiah 5.1–7), and Jesus used these
images in various ways in his teaching about the Kingdom of God.
Our Creator has made the earth to be naturally fruitful: it is a sign of
His overflowing bounty. The mysterious process of fertile growth is
God's gift: a tree, or a vine, or a field of corn will naturally bear fruit
in its season. Our part is to wait patiently, and to trust that God's
watchful care will protect His precious crop from being pillaged or
choked by weeds. God's indiscriminate generosity, lavished on all His
creatures, often seems scandalous to our mean spirits, as Jesus shows
in his parable of the vineyard-workers (Matthew 20.1–16). In
Chapter 15 of St John's Gospel Jesus is himself the Vine, and we are
its fruit-bearing branches. Often we do not seem to be bearing fruit at
all, but, if we remain united with him by prayer and sacrament, he
assures us that the fruit will come and that it will last.

Numquam deseras, a daily blessing at the end of Matins, BR p. 51.

(Sundays in Ordinary Time continue after Trinity)

Sunday next before Lent (Transfiguration Sunday)

A glimpse of glory

Jesus took with him Peter, James, and John as his witnesses;
he went up the mountain,
and in the presence of Moses and Elijah
the appearance of his human body was transfigured
and his splendour and glory were seen.

Suddenly, a great light shone around him;
his face became like the shining sun,
and his clothes were white as the snow.

All who saw the miracle were amazed.
A bright cloud overshadowed them
and the Father's voice sounded from heaven:
'This is my Son, my only Beloved;
in him I am well pleased,
and, in him, all things are pleasing to me.'

Rejoice, you faithful company of Christians who trust in God;
by sharing the sufferings of Christ, you will reign with him in
     glory.
Every tear shall be wiped away from the eyes of his holy ones;
the just shall be joyful and shine with light everlasting.

Moses and Elijah both encountered God on mountain-tops, and they
represent the partial revelation of God through Law and Prophecy.
Now they give place to the fuller manifestation of His glory in the
person of His beloved Son. This poet, probably PETER THE VENER-
ABLE, Abbot of Cluny (d. 1156), sees the Transfiguration as a
promise of glory for all Creation. As His adopted sons and daughters,
the Father delights in us, and makes us heirs of the glory of heaven.

Assumpsit Petri, from the Sequence *Fulget mundo*, LS p. 48.
     The Feast of the Transfiguration has been observed in the eastern
church since the late fourth century, but it was slow to catch on in the
west. Its earliest western Mass-texts are in the Spanish-Roman Vich
Sacramentary which dates from 1038. Peter the Venerable was a great
enthusiast for the feast, and *Fulget mundo* is among the texts
appended to the Office- and Mass-Propers which he compiled.
Observance of the Feast was made compulsory for all Cluniac houses

in 1132, and the influence of Cluny led to its gradual spread throughout Europe. It was only in the fifteenth century, however, that non-monastic churches adopted the feast; its Mass-texts were often added to missals in an appendix along with those of other new feasts such as the Visitation and the Holy Name.

Kehrein, the editor of LS, takes the text of *Fulget mundo* from a fifteenth-century Einsiedeln missal. In England and France custom-made Transfiguration Sequences were rare: English Mass-books usually have either *Benedicta semper* from Trinity Sunday, or Notker's Easter Sequence *Laudes salvatori*; in France, the Royal Abbey of St Denis in Paris had Stephen Langton's Pentecost Sequence *Veni sancte spiritus*. *Fulget mundo* is, however, found in three English manuscripts: the Ordinal of the Benedictine nunnery of Barking in Essex (1394–1404), a fifteenth-century Breviary from Arlingham in Gloucestershire, and a Sarum Gradual of similar date, also from the neighbourhood of Gloucester.

For more details see R. W. Pfaff, *New Liturgical Feasts in Later Medieval England* (Oxford 1970), Chapter 2.

Lent

Ash Wednesday

A blessing of ashes

Almighty and eternal God,
You have mercy on all Your creatures,
and hate nothing which You have made.
You overlook Your people's sins because of their repentance,
and You come to help those who are struggling in any kind of
   need.

Graciously bless and sanctify these ashes,
which, following the example of the people of Nineveh,
we are to place upon our heads
as a sign of our faith and humility,
and for the purging of our sins.

We call upon Your name,
and pray that all who bear them upon their heads and ask for
   Your mercy
may receive pardon for all their sins,
and so make a good beginning today to their Lenten observance.

On the Day of Resurrection
may they be worthy to draw near with pure hearts to Your holy
   Paschal Feast,
and in the world to come may they be crowned with eternal
   glory,
through Christ our Lord.

This was one of the prayers used in medieval England at the ceremony
of the blessing and imposition of ashes which took place before Mass.
Ashes are an age-old symbol of humility and sorrow (e.g. Jonah 3.6);
they represent our sorrow at the ways in which we hurt God and
other people. The prayer ends, however, on a note of hope: it points
forward to the goal of Lenten observance, the celebration of Easter,
and to our sharing an eternal Easter in heaven. Repentance should
lead on to trust in God's mercy and to the hope of glory.

Omnipotens sempiterne, SM p. 50.
   Originally, ashes were only placed on the heads of those doing

public penance, who were then excluded from church until their solemn re-admission on Maundy Thursday, but by the tenth century this penitential rite involved the whole congregation.

This prayer occurs in both Sarum and York Uses. Like Cranmer's Ash Wednesday Collect in the *Book of Common Prayer*, it incorporates phrases from the Introit of the Mass ('You have mercy on all Your creatures, and hate nothing which You have made') which are in turn quoted from Wisdom of Solomon 11.23–24.

First Sunday of Lent

The bread of God

Holy Father, as we take up our Lenten discipline, Your only Son, who lives in Your glory, nourishes our faith, increases our hope, and strengthens our love. He is the true and living bread, which came down from heaven, and yet remains in heaven for ever. He is the very substance of eternity and the food of virtue. For Your Word, by whom all things were made, is both the bread of our human spirits and also the bread of angels.

Your servant Moses was nourished by this bread for forty days and forty nights before he was given the Law. He fasted and abstained from bodily food, so that he might be more open to receive Your sweetness. The sweetness of Your word lived in his spirit, and its light shone in his face. His body felt no hunger, and he forgot earthly food, because he gazed on the brightness of Your glory, and was fed by Your word.

Throughout these forty days, O Lord, graciously give us this bread.

The author of this prayer from seventh-century France is meditating on Jesus' fasting and temptation in the wilderness. He compares Jesus' fast to that of Moses, whom he imagines as being so intent on being with God that he was oblivious of earthly food. The people of Israel put God their Father to the test and lusted for bread in the wilderness. Jesus, the New Israel and true Son of God, overcame this temptation and trusted God, in accordance with the saying in Deuteronomy 8.3 'Man shall not live by bread alone, but by every word that proceeds from the mouth of God' (Matthew 4.4). The author of the prayer reflects that Jesus is himself the Word of God, and that he said, in John 6.51, 'I am the living bread which came down from heaven; if any one eats of this bread, he will live for ever.'

Filius tuus, the *Immolatio* (Proper Preface) for the beginning of Lent in the *Missale Gothicum* (see p. 26), MG p. 51.
    The *Missale Gothicum* comes from a time when Lent still began on this Sunday. The Gelasian Sacramentary, which spread from Rome to Gaul during the eighth century, provides the first evidence for Lent

beginning on Ash Wednesday. The extra days were added in order to bring the number of actual fast-days before Easter up to forty. Sundays, even in Lent, were regarded in Rome as feast-days.

Second Sunday of Lent

(If today's Gospel is an account of the Transfiguration, see **Sunday next before Lent**, *A glimpse of glory*, p. 52.)

A true fast

In this our Lenten fast, O Lord, remember Your mercies
which You have always shown to penitent sinners.
May we offer You a fast which is pleasing to You,
abstaining not just from food, but also from all our sins,
so that our desires and intentions may be in accordance with
  Your will.

Sin and strife beset our mortal nature, O Lord;
be present with us,
and grant that the medicine of our Lenten discipline may
  cleanse us,
and enable us to love one another in sincerity of heart,
through Christ our Lord.

The author of this prayer sees that fasting and other forms of Lenten discipline are not ends in themselves. Indeed they have the potential of leading us into spiritual danger: managing to keep our Lenten rule can leave us feeling self-satisfied and superior, while failing to keep it may bring us to an equally unhealthy state of despair. The proper use of self-denial is as a means to an end: it is a cleansing medicine which helps us to sift out of the mixture of our lives what our true priorities are. It clarifies our vision, so that we can see what is really important to us. This can sometimes result in a humbling realization of just how much we want our own way! We fear that loving God and other people will diminish us and wear us away to nothing. The reverse, of course, is true: the more we give, the more we receive. As we try to align our wills with God's will (the goal of all Lenten discipline), we discover that He wants us to be fully ourselves and to have life in all its abundance.

Memento Domine, the *Immolatio* from the second Lenten Mass, and *Praesta*, the prayer at the Kiss of Peace (*Collectio ad Pacem*) from the following Mass in the *Missale Gothicum* (see p. 26), MG pp. 55–56.

In the Gallican Rite the exchanging of the Peace was introduced by a prayer appropriate to the theme of each particular Mass.

Third Sunday of Lent

The stream of love

His body hung upon the cross,
his lifeless arms stretched wide,
no longer feeling pain; but when
a soldier pierced his side,
the spear transfixed his mother's heart;
in agony she cried,
and saw the blood and water flow
forth from the Crucified.

Let all those who search for love,
healing, and salvation,
hasten to this stream and drink
from its rich libation.
Precious blood, which from our ills
brings us liberation;
living water, clear and sweet,
fount of new creation.

This fifteenth-century poet is meditating on the final scene of the drama of the Crucifixion as told in John 19.34. The stream flowing from Jesus' pierced side is a vivid symbol of the compassion and love which flow from the heart of God. This is the living water, welling up to eternal life, which Jesus had promised to the Samaritan woman in John 4.14. Like the stream issuing from the right side of the temple in Ezekiel 47, it brings new life wherever it flows. St John emphasizes the paradox that the source of this joyful life is a scene of suffering and death: the lifting up of Christ on the cross is his exaltation and triumph. St Paul too knows how God's vulnerable love revealed on Calvary can conquer proud human hearts: the weakness and humiliation of Christ crucified is the power and wisdom of God (I Corinthians 1.24).

Corpus quidem, part of the Sequence *Cenam cum discipulis*, LS p. 64.
    This Sequence is found in manuscripts from St Gall and Einsiedeln, and became widespread in England and northern Europe. Its earliest appearance in England is probably in a Sarum missal thought to have been written for the monks of Durham in the first half of the fifteenth century (Oxford, Bodl. MS. Laud misc. 302). It was commonly used at the Mass of the Five Wounds, a devotion which originated in

Germany (Fritzlar in Thuringia has been suggested) and became very popular in the later Middle Ages. Like the cultus of the Holy Name, it belongs to that tradition of warm, affective devotion to Christ in his Sacred Humanity which spread through western Christendom during and after the twelfth century, due in large part to the influence of St Bernard and the Cistercians. After the thirteenth century, under Franciscan influence, this devotion was especially focused on aspects of the Passion. In Germany the Five Wounds cultus became a liturgical feast, but in England it remained as a Votive Mass, usually celebrated on a Friday as an alternative to the Mass of the Holy Cross.

R. W. Pfaff (see p. 53) discusses this Mass on pp. 84–91 of *New Liturgical Feasts*.

Fourth Sunday of Lent (Mothering Sunday)

The cost of motherhood: Mary at the Cross

'Why should you suffer like this, my sweetest son?
You have never done any wrong;
why should you die nailed to a cross, as if you were a criminal?
How can I go on living, when my son endures such pain?
Is this the grace which you brought to me, Gabriel,
when you said "Hail Mary, full of grace"?
I have the very opposite of what you promised me:
instead of grace, I have pain and punishment.
You called me the most blessed of all women;
now, my grief and affliction are plain for all to see'.

Beside the cross she stands, weeping and lamenting,
as from the gibbet the body of her Son is lifted down.
There stands the Mother, desolate;
deprived of her motherhood, bereft of her own sweet Son.

Mother of Jesus, by the sufferings which you bore with your
    Son,
grant that our hearts may be pierced with the sword of
    compassion.
After the griefs of this life, may we come, with you, to share
    eternal joys.

On this day of thanksgiving and prayer for mothers (whether on earth
or in Paradise), it is good to remember with compassion those for
whom Mothering Sunday brings not just happy memories, but also
painful ones: all those whose children have died or are estranged from
them. In this fifteenth-century poem Mary is not afraid to give vent to
the anger which is a common element in grief and which we are so
often ashamed to express. Mother Julian (see p. 48) said of Mary 'She
and Christ were so one in their love that the greatness of her love
caused the greatness of her suffering' (*op. cit.* p. 91). Grief is the
shadow-side of love, a shadow which will fade in the dawning light of
Easter.

Fili dulcissime, part of the Sequence *Maestae parentis Christi*, LS
p. 180.
   The first appearance of this Sequence in England is in the edition of
the Sarum Missal printed in Rouen in 1497. It is set for the Mass of

the Compassion or Lamentation of Blessed Mary, one of the supple-
mentary Masses at the end of the book.

R. W. Pfaff (see p. 53) has a section on this Mass in *New Liturgical Feasts* pp. 97–103.

Fifth Sunday of Lent (Passiontide)

The altar of the Cross

To you, O Christ, be endless praises,
new and fresh as the springtime;
to you be radiant glory;
as David sang in his psalm,
you shone before the rising of the morning star.

Mighty Word of God,
in your merciful kindness you took upon yourself our humanity.
The altar of the Cross bore you up,
that holy altar which brought cleansing to the world,
and through which the Church, your glorious offspring, was
    brought to birth.

The Church prays that, through the wounds of your Cross
and your rose-red streams,
you will fill all the children she bears you
with the grace which flows from heaven.

Defend them with faith,
that they may overcome evil,
and may rejoice for ever in your starry palace,
sharing the crown of your Godhead.

From all eternity Christ's whole being is an outpouring of love to the
Father, from his begetting 'before the morning star' (Psalm
109[110].3, Vulgate), in every moment of his incarnate life, and
supremely when that life was offered on the altar of the Cross.
Christ's streaming wounds remind this poet of the blood and water
which flow in the act of giving birth: his sufferings are the birth-pangs
of the Church, the Bride who in every generation will bear him children nourished by the streams of grace which flow from him.

Sit laus vernans from the Sequence *Gloria resonante* (in honour of the
Holy Cross) in the Winchester Troper, YM p. 306.
  In the tenth century Winchester was the capital of the kingdom of
Wessex, where Alfred had begun a brave revival of the Christian
culture which had been ravaged by the Viking invasions of the ninth
century. His work was consolidated by King Athelstan and by the
monastic reformers Dunstan and Aethelwold. The troper from which

this Sequence comes was used in the New Minster at Winchester built by Bishop Aethelwold. The manuscript dates from the last years of the tenth century.

The Sequence is typical of the Winchester school in its use of flowery language and compound words – rather like the work of a schoolboy showing off recently-acquired knowledge. Nevertheless it has some striking imagery and a certain charm. It does not seem to have been used outside its home territory.

Palm Sunday

Welcoming the King

We praise you, Lord, and share in your triumph on this solemn
    day
when great crowds of people from Jerusalem and Bethany went
    out to meet you
and with one voice cried out 'Hosanna to the Son of David!
Blessed is he who comes in the name of the Lord!'

They paid you homage not just with their tongues,
but also with leafy boughs from the trees:
your sandy pathway became green with the branches which they
    laid there.
The people spread their cloaks at your feet,
stripping themselves to clothe your path,
and preparing a triumph for their new hero.
The clamour of voices shouting their praise reached into the
    temple,
as they cried 'Blessed is he who comes in the name of the Lord!'

Look, Jerusalem, and see how your king comes to you
in meekness, sitting upon an ass.

Come then, Lord, and be present in our midst.
You have restored us by your Cross:
raise up again now all who have fallen.
Let us go to meet you, knowing that you have come to our
    hearts,
and let us praise you with the angel-host of heaven.

The author of this prayer sees the paradox that as we welcome Christ
our King, who comes to us in gentleness and humility, we know that
he has already come to our hearts, else we should not be seeking him.
With each passing year, we look on the events of Holy Week from a
slightly different perspective, like looking at the view as we climb a
spiral staircase. We have moved on since last year and are ready to
encounter new aspects of the mystery of God's love.

Tibi Domine, the *Immolatio* for Palm Sunday in the *Missale
Gothicum* (see p. 26) MG p. 61.

The Blessing and Procession of Palms was one of the legacies bequeathed to the Roman Rite by the Gallican church, though it had formed part of the liturgy of Jerusalem since the fourth century. In the towns and villages of medieval Europe the ceremony was a dramatic event involving the whole community. When the palms, green branches, or flowers had been blessed, the procession went out to a cross in the churchyard where the Palm Sunday story was read or sung. The people waited by the cross as another procession, in which a symbol of Christ was carried, came out to meet them. In England this was a procession of the Blessed Sacrament, which was carried beneath a silken canopy, while in Germany it included a figure of Christ mounted on a wooden donkey on wheels, called the *Palmesel*. The combined procession then moved to the south side of the church where, from a specially-built platform, seven boys sang Theodulf of Orléans' hymn 'All glory, laud, and honour'. There was a dramatic entry into church, representing Christ's entry into Jerusalem, and then the great crucifix on the Rood Screen, which had been veiled all through Lent, was uncovered and the anthem 'Hail, our King' was sung. The rich variety of words, music, movement, drama, and visual imagery enabled everyone, whatever their level of education, to participate in celebrating the mystery of Redemption in the liturgy of Holy Week.

For more details see E. Duffy, *The Stripping of the Altars* (Yale 1992), pp. 23–27.

Maundy Thursday

The washing of feet

The Lord Jesus Christ girded himself with a towel
and washed the feet of his disciples;
as he was about to leave this world, he left them this example
    of humility.
The teacher of truth had often instructed them in the way of
    salvation;
now he taught them by his deeds.

It was fitting that he should gird himself with a towel,
since he had taken upon himself the form of a servant
and wore the robe of our humanity.
It was fitting that he should pour water into a bowl
to wash the disciples' feet,
since he was to pour out his blood upon the earth
to wash away the stains of our sins.
Those feet, which he washed and wiped with a towel,
were to go about spreading his gospel and bearing witness to
    him.
As he outwardly washed their feet, he inwardly cleansed their
    souls,
sprinkling them with the hyssop of his pardon.

O great and wonderful mystery!
Peter was troubled, seeing this act of such great humility.
His human nature trembled in fear before the great King's
    majesty,
for God Himself was graciously bending low at his feet.
But if God had not stooped down in humility to human beings,
humanity would never have been raised up
to stand at full height in God's presence.

In this meditation on the story of Jesus washing his disciples' feet (John 13.1–15) Christ's action is seen as a symbol of the Incarnation itself, in which the Divine Son took on the form of a servant (Philippians 2.5–11).

Qui suorum pedes, the *Immolatio* for Maundy Thursday in the *Missale Gothicum* (see p. 26), MG p. 63.

The ceremony of the Footwashing is first found at the end of the seventh century in Spain; the conservative Roman Rite did not adopt it until the twelfth century. 'Maundy' is a corruption of *Mandatum*, the opening of the first antiphon sung during the ceremony: 'A new commandment I give to you, that you love one another as I have loved you' (John 13.34). The last antiphon *Congregavit nos*, with its refrain *Ubi caritas*, is part of a poem by Charlemagne's friend Paulinus of Aquileia. It is translated below in Part III, under 'Stewardship Renewal'.

Good Friday

Our ransom

When the world's maker
suffered the penalty of death on a cross,
he cried out with a loud voice,
and breathed out his Spirit.

The temple-veil was torn in two, and graves opened,
for there had been a great earthquake:
the world was crying out
that it could not bear the death of God's own Son.

When a soldier with his spear
opened the side of our crucified Lord,
there flowed out blood and water
for our healing and redemption.

This is our ransom-price, whose weight
wonderfully sets free the world's captivity,
destroys the dark dungeons of death,
and opens to us the door of the kingdom.

The image of the death of Christ as a ransom-price can, like any analogy, become misleading if pressed too far. It does not mean that God demanded a blood-letting to appease His anger at human sin. The Cross is what it cost Jesus to live a totally dedicated life in union with his Father's will. His death was the final act of a life which reveals the depth of God's love for us. It sets us free because the impact on us of that life and death opens up our self-centred hearts so that they can receive and rejoice in God's limitless love, and can begin to reflect some of that love to others. He has opened for us the door of the kingdom and his grace helps us enter into it more and more fully.

Dum fabricator, SM p. 114.

In medieval England this antiphon was sung by the choir while the people expressed their love for Christ by approaching the cross and kissing it. It followed the singing of the Reproaches ('O my people'), which accompanied the Veneration of the Cross by the clergy.

Like the Palm Sunday Procession, the Veneration of the Cross was a feature of the Holy Week liturgy at Jerusalem in the fourth century. It was known in seventh-century Gaul and passed into the Roman Rite during the Carolingian Period.

Good Friday

Conqueror of Death

Christ became a meek victim, offered for our healing.
Bearing the humiliations of the Cross,
he who is Eternal Life consented to die.

He drained the cup of bitter gall,
and suffered grievous wounds,
his flesh pierced through by nails and spear.

In suffering thus, he freed us from our sins,
and, descending to the lowest realms of death,
disarmed our ancient foe.

On the third day he returned in his victorious might;
he bore with him the trophy of his triumph over death:
our human flesh, risen in glory.

As well as the bodily sufferings endured by Jesus on the Cross, this
poet points to his inner sufferings, his humiliations. These included
not just the cruel mockery from the bystanders, but also the sense that
his whole life's work was ending in failure. There was the hurt caused
by being deserted by his friends, and even being betrayed by one of
them; then there was the deeper spiritual agony of feeling abandoned
by God. In solidarity with his fellow human beings he experienced the
humiliating breakdown of body, mind, and spirit which preceded his
encounter with death, the last enemy of us all. But the poet also points
us forward to Easter, God's turning upside-down of this apparent
humiliation and defeat and His making it into a triumphant victory
over death for all humanity. The God who brought Creation out of
nothing can bring good out of evil and life from death.

Christus namque from the Sequence *Concinat orbis*, SM p. 468.
   This tenth-century Sequence was sung in many parts of Europe in
Easter week. Its melody was called *Cignea* or *Pascha nostrum*, after
the Easter Alleluia-verse 'Christ our Passover is sacrificed for us' on
which the music is based. The York Use and some Sarum manuscripts
assign it to Easter Wednesday; other Sarum books set it for Tuesday.
It survived to appear in many French and English printed missals,
including the Sarum one produced in Mary's reign in 1554.

Good Friday

Mary's grief

O my Son, my only sweetness, and my special joy,
look upon your mother's tears, and bring me some comfort.

Your wounds torment my eyes, my mind, and my heart.
What mother, what woman has ever known such joy as I knew,
and such misery?

In your pain, the colour drains from your face;
it rushes and floods down in a tide of blood.

Oh, the gentleness of your heart, suffering such pain!
Oh, the goodness of your grace, dying so meekly!

How true the words of faithful Simeon:
now I feel within me that sword of grief which he promised;
my sobbing, my sighs, and my tears
are the outward signs of my inner wound.

O Sion's children, run into his arms,
as he hangs upon the cross;
those arms are there outstretched,
ready to embrace all those who love him.

The author of this lament is GODFREY OF BRETEUIL (d. 1196),
who was Sub-prior of the Augustinian abbey of St Victor in Paris.
Godfrey's poetic imagination enables us to share something of Mary's
grief at the foot of the cross; despite her grief, he sees her as inviting
all Christians to respond to the love revealed in her Son's outstretched
arms, as he lays down his life for his friends.

Fili dulcor unice from *Planctus ante nescia* in F. Gennrich's (succinctly
entitled!) *Grundriss einer Formenlehre des mittelalterlichen Liedes als
Grundlage einer musikalischen Formenlehre des Liedes* (Halle 1932,
republished Tübingen 1970) p. 143.
   The suffering of Mary at the Cross was a favourite subject of late
medieval devotion (see pp. 61–62), but Godfrey's Sequence shows
that in the twelfth century it was already an element in Victorine spir-
ituality (see pp. 12 and 16).

Planctus ante nescia is an example of a 'Da Capo Sequence' or 'Sequence with double cursus'. This means that part of the normal melodic pattern (consisting of progressive repetition AA, BB, CC, etc.) was repeated in the course of the piece, so that the first six stanzas of this Sequence have the structure AA, BB, CC, BB, CC, DD. This was not an invention of the Victorines: as early as the ninth century Sequences were displaying this sort of complex patterning. One of them, *Rex caeli*, was sufficiently well-known to be quoted as an example of various musical intervals in the handbook *Musica enchiriadis* (text in Gerbert [see p. 18] *Scriptores*, pp. 155 and 169). Some scholars, for example Peter Dronke in *The Medieval Lyric* (London 1968) p. 39, believe that Sequences must have originated before the ninth century in order to have achieved the level of sophistication shown in *Rex caeli* by the 850s. But this view both ignores the evidence of Amalarius of Metz (early 830s), for whom the term '*sequentia*' still meant a wordless melody following the Alleluia, and also seriously underestimates the extent of the creativity unleashed by the Carolingian Renaissance.

Planctus ante nescia does not seem to have been used liturgically even at St Victor itself.

Good Friday

Adoration of Christ Crucified

Lord Jesus Christ,
we adore you as you are lifted up on the cross;
we pray that your cross may free us from the assaults of evil.

We adore you as you are wounded upon the cross;
we pray that those wounds may be a healing medicine for our
    souls.

We adore you as you are laid in the tomb;
we pray that your death may be our life.

We adore you as you descend to the lowest regions of the dead
to free those held captive;
we pray that you will never allow us to enter there.

We adore you as you rise from the dead and ascend to heaven;
we pray you to have mercy upon us.

We adore you who are to come as our judge;
we pray that at your coming you will not enter into judgement
    with us sinners,
but we ask that, before you judge us, you will forgive us.

For you live and reign with God the Father
in the unity of the Holy Spirit,
world without end.

These tenth-century Anglo-Saxon prayers lead us from contemplating
Jesus on the Cross to the consequences of his victory over death: the
liberation of the dead of former ages – the Harrowing ('raking-out')
of Hell was a favourite theme of medieval iconography – and our own
hope of mercy and resurrection.

Domine Jesu Christe, PC p. 143.
   These were the prayers used in Anglo-Saxon England during the
Veneration of the Cross on Good Friday. They are found *c.* 970 in the
Regularis concordia, which embodies the monastic reforms of St
Aethelwold, Bishop of Winchester (see p. 63), and in this early
eleventh-century manuscript from Winchester's 'Nunnaminster' they

are followed by an Anglo-Saxon translation for the benefit of those nuns who did not know Latin. The manuscript (B. L. Cotton Galba A. xiv), which was damaged in a fire at Ashburnham House in 1731, looks as if it was a nun's exercise-book. It contains some interesting Celtic pieces, for example Columba's poem *Altus prosator*, and a version of the Offertory prayer *Suscipe sancta Trinitas* which is considerably longer than that included in the Tridentine Missal. Though a prayer to be said by the priest at the altar, it is here in the feminine gender, so was clearly used by the nuns in their own devotions.

Holy Saturday

The new fire

O Lord our God, Father Almighty,
Light unfailing, and Creator of all light,
hear us your servants and bless this fire,
so that it may be hallowed by Your holy benediction,
for You enlighten everyone who comes into this world.

Enlighten our hearts and consciences with the fire of Your love.
May Your fire enkindle us,
and Your light shine upon us.
Drive from our hearts the darkness of sin,
and lead us by Your radiance into Your eternal life.

As the new fire springs up from the striking of a flint, so the risen life
of Christ springs up from the rock of the sepulchre. The firelight scat-
tering the darkness of Easter Eve reminds this prayer's author of Jesus
the Light of the World, as described in the prologue to St John's
Gospel (1.4–9). The darkness of death has not overcome that light: it
burns with the fire of God's love, and seeks to enkindle an answering
love in our hearts.

As the pillar of fire led the Israelites out of slavery and towards the
Promised Land, so the Easter Candle, lit from the new fire, symbol-
izes the presence of the Risen Christ with his people as he leads them
away from the bondage of sin and death, and towards the glory of
heaven.

Domine Deus, the Blessing of the New Fire in the Sarum Missal, SM
p. 115.

A version of this prayer was in the Tridentine Missal and was used
in the Roman Rite until the Holy Week Liturgy was revised in 1955.
Another variant appears in the medieval Sarum Use at the Blessing of
Candles at Candlemas.

Medieval Christians had a great flair for drama, and this was put to
especially good use in the arrangements for lighting the Paschal
Candle. In Durham Cathedral the candle-stand itself reached as high
as the triforium and occupied almost the whole width of the choir.
Upon it was placed a piece of wood as high as a man, and on top of
that was the Paschal Candle. It was so high that it had to be lit by
means of a device lowered from the roof! Details are in R. W. J.
Austin, *The Rites of Durham* (Durham n. d.) p. 8; this is a selection

in modern English of the full text, which has been edited by J. T. Fowler (Surtees Society 1902). The book consists of reminiscences, dating from 1593, of the life, worship, and furnishings of the Cathedral Priory before the Reformation.

The Easter Vigil ceremonies are treated very thoroughly in Alistair Macgregor, *Fire and Light in the Western Triduum* (Collegeville 1992).

Holy Saturday

The Alleluia returns

'Tell us, Alleluia, as you visit our land again,
from what regions have you come,
with your message of new joys for all the world?'

The smiling Alleluia replied in her sweet voice:
'An angel from Christ showed holy wonders to me;
with a voice full of praise,
he sang that the Lord of the stars had risen.

On the wings of a bird I quickly flew through the empty air,
and gladly came back to you, his servants.
I come to tell you that the old Law is empty and void,
and the new kingdom of Grace is here.

Christ willingly took death upon himself,
so that he might save us from eternal death.
Now all creatures can take their rest
and enjoy fullness of life without end.

Servants of Christ, join with me now
to celebrate his holy Passover with praise and rejoicing.
Christ is our peace.'

Since Septuagesima, three weeks before Lent, the joyful Alleluia-chant
had disappeared from the Church's liturgy. Now, at the Easter Vigil
Mass, it returns; this ninth-century poet personifies the Alleluia,
making her a messenger of Easter joy. The emptiness of the air
through which she flies is an image of the emptiness of the Law, now
that the Risen Christ has brought in his kingdom of grace and peace,
in which all Creation can rejoice.

Alleluia dic nobis, SM p. 468.
This Sequence is found in the early collections from Limoges and
Winchester and was sung all over Europe at Easter. It occurs in 17
English uses: at Sarum it was set for Easter Wednesday, at York for
Saturday. At Winchester its melody was called *Angelica*; elsewhere it
was known as *Nobilissima* or *Romana*. Notker used the tune for two
of his Sequences, *Laurenti David* (translated below in Part II under
Feasts of Martyrs), and *Johannes Jesu* (translated in *Paths of the
Heart*, p. 86).

Easter

Easter Day

The joy of new life

This day's radiant splendour shines throughout the world;
today the tale of Christ's glorious victory is told with joy.

Eternal King, as you sit at the Father's right hand,
receive our praises with your loving kindness.

You are the conqueror of death for all your creatures,
and in your triumph you possess the joys of heaven.

Praise and honour and might are yours,
for you have lifted from us our ancient burden.

Redeemed by the rose-red blood of the merciful Lamb,
this earth, our dwelling-place, glows bright with flowers;
it offers them as pure and gleaming gifts to you,
for in your strength and goodness you have washed away our
  sins.

This day's fame resounds throughout the ages,
for today the life of the world rises again.
His loving kindness has made us rich
with the firm hope that, after this life,
we shall rise again and live for ever.

This poet sees the new life which sprang from the Easter sepulchre as
embracing the whole of God's Creation. The spring flowers, whose
colours brighten the earth, share in the joy of resurrection. The
ancient burden of our bondage to sin and death has been lifted; God's
grace has made us truly rich by giving us the hope of eternal life.

Selected verses from *Fulgens praeclara*, SM p. 467.
   This tenth-century Sequence was sung throughout England and
France on Easter Day. It also occurs in many German and Italian
manuscripts. It incorporates an earlier partial text beginning *Rex in
aeternum*; this consists of three pairs of verses set to part of the third,
seventh and eleventh phrases of the melody. It is possible that these
partially-texted Sequences represent a first phase in the development

of the *genre*, a half-way stage between pure melody and melody provided with a full text. The evidence, however, is inconclusive, since partially-texted Sequences occur no earlier in the manuscript tradition than fully-texted ones.

The last stanza of the translation is *Nam resultet* from the Sequence *Jubilans concrepa*, YM p. 312.

This is also tenth-century and was probably written at Winchester, where its melody was called *Vaga varia*. It is also found at Westminster, Chichester, Dublin, Rouen and in a Templar manuscript. Some Sarum books also include it. The day when it was performed varied between the Thursday, Friday and Saturday of Easter week.

Second Sunday of Easter

The upper room

Your only Son, O God,
graciously appeared today to his disciples when the doors were
    shut;
may he fill us with the precious gift of his blessing,
and open to us the doors of the kingdom of heaven.

He took away from the disciples' hearts
the doubt which was wounding them,
by letting them touch his body;
may he take away from us the scars of our sins,
through our faith in his Resurrection.

With Thomas we believe that he is our Lord and our God,
and we call upon him in humble faith;
may he keep us safe from all evil in this world,
and enable us to stand in the company of saints in the world
    to come.

The Resurrection has let Christ loose upon the world: he can enter
even those places where the doors are barred and bolted to keep out
whatever is unfamiliar and threatening. In the midst of the fear which
filled that upper room where the disciples were assembled, the Risen
Jesus made himself known and gave his Easter gift of peace.

This prayer asks Jesus, who shares our wounded humanity, to heal
the inner wounds which diminish our lives. He ministers to us according to our needs: he accepted Thomas' honest doubts and gave him
the reassurance he needed, so that he was able to go on to doubt his
doubts and say 'My Lord and my God'. Doubt is part of the process
of achieving a mature relationship with God; the presence of Christ,
who lovingly accepts us as we are, gives us the courage to open more
of ourselves to him, and allows fear to melt into faith.

Deus cuius, the Blessing for Low Sunday in the Benedictional of
Archbishop Robert (see p. 20), BR p. 18.

Third Sunday of Easter

Meeting the Risen Christ

Brightly shines the day which was made by the Lord;
Christ the conqueror, destroying death,
shows himself alive to his beloved friends:
first to Mary, then to the apostles.
He teaches them the scriptures,
opening their hearts,
that things which once were hidden
now through him should be revealed.

The God of surprises reveals His Son to us in unexpected ways, often while we are doing ordinary things: going on a journey and having a meal, like the two disciples on the road to Emmaus, or going about our work, like the disciples fishing on the lake. Meeting Jesus and keeping company with him has the effect on us of opening up our hearts and minds. It makes us more ready to recognize him in the scriptures and in the Breaking of Bread (as the Eucharist was often called in the early Church).

NOTKER suggests in this poem that the Risen Christ can open our hearts to other things as well: perhaps to uncomfortable truths about ourselves which we had kept hidden but can now bring out into the open, trusting in God's merciful love. Beside a fire at Jerusalem Peter had thrice denied Christ; now by the fire at the lakeside (John 21) the wounds of his shame are healed by his triple affirmation of love. The early Christians loved to find significance in numbers, and the mention of 153 fish may be a subtle link with the earlier lakeside feeding in John 6: there the superabundant bread was counted out (5 loaves + 12 baskets of fragments = 17), here the superabundant fish is counted – a triangular net with 17 fish at the bottom would, when full, contain 153 (17+16+15 etc.). The link shows that the mysterious figure on the shore is the Jesus the disciples knew, being typically generous in his unexpected provision of food.

Illuxit dies, part of the Sequence *Laudes salvatori* by Notker (see pp. 24 & 25), NP p. 28.
Another part of this Sequence is translated above on p. 36.

Fourth Sunday of Easter

The Good Shepherd

When the world began, O God, You subdued the waves of the
   sea,
and made the earth fertile with plants of every kind.

Grant, O Good Shepherd, that we your flock,
who celebrate your Resurrection,
may be led into the pastures of eternal life.

Watch over your sheep and lambs, and protect them;
may none fall victim to the attacks of the wolf
and be carried off as his prey.

Rescue us from the jaws of the wolf,
and make us worthy to feast among the flowers of Paradise.

The God who created the earth's green pastures and refreshing
streams is our Creator too; He knows all our needs and cares for us
with infinite love. In the psalms and prophets God's care for His
people is likened to that of a shepherd looking after his flock, as in
Isaiah's verse 'He will feed his flock like a shepherd, he will gather the
lambs in his arms, he will carry them in his bosom, and gently lead
those that are with young' (40.11). In *The Crown of the Year*
(London 1952, p. 30), Austin Farrer wrote 'Christ's parable of the
shepherd escapes us not by being obscure, but by being so plain. The
meaning is so familiar that we overlook it. What does he say? A man
cares naturally for his own things. He does not have to make himself
care ... Christ cares for us as no one else can, because we are his. We
do not belong to any other man; we belong to him. His dying for us
in this world is the natural effect of his unique care. It is the act of our
Creator'. Christ our God, who feeds us with a shepherd's care, loves
us so much that he is prepared to lay down his own life so that we
may have life in all its abundance.

Deus qui inter, the blessing for the Saturday in Easter Week in the
Benedictional of Archbishop Robert (see p. 20), BR p. 18.

Fifth Sunday of Easter

Year A: See Second Sunday of Epiphany, Year B, *Following God's way*, p. 26.

Year B: *The True Vine*

> Let Christ's Church sing a love-song for her Beloved,
> because he, her God, left his home
> and clothed himself in our human nature.
>
> Her sacraments flowed from your sacred side, O Christ,
> as you hung upon the cross;
> by the help of your cross may she be kept safe
> in the flowing tides of time.
>
> Beneath your pleasant vine
> the whole Church plays in peace.
> You rose from the dead in a garden,
> and you open up to your people
> the flowery garden of Paradise
> which had long been closed to them,
> Lord and King of kings.

In this poem NOTKER'S imagination is working with two Old Testament passages about vines: Isaiah 5.1 'Let me sing for my beloved a love-song concerning his vineyard', and Micah's vision of peace and security under God's protection in 4.4 'They shall sit every man under his vine and under his fig tree, and none shall make them afraid'. But the security which allows us to 'play in peace' comes at a cost to God. We are kept safe amid the ebb and flow of our lives because Christ made himself so vulnerable that his very blood flowed out of him on the Cross. The True Vine fills with his own life-blood the chalice from which we drink eternal life; because of the Resurrection, God's vineyard is also the Garden of Paradise.

Selected verses from *Carmen suo dilecto* by Notker (see pp. 24–25), NP p. 38.
 Notker set this Sequence in his *Liber hymnorum* for the Saturday in Easter week. Its melody was known as *Pascha* or *Amoena*. As well as at Notker's own abbey of St Gall, it was sung during the eleventh century at Prüm and Echternach. It seems not to have survived into

the later Middle Ages: it is absent, for instance, from the early four-teenth-century repertoire of the Cistercians of Kaisheim-bei-Donauwörth, and it was not known in England or France.

Fifth Sunday of Easter

Year C: *Christ who creates us anew*

Christ our God has washed us with water from his side
and has redeemed us by pouring out his blood;
may he strengthen within us the grace of redemption
which we have received.

Through him we have been born again
by water and the Holy Spirit;
may he grant us a share in his heavenly kingdom.

He has enabled us to begin our journey of faith;
may he also complete his work in us,
and bring us to the full perfection of love.

May the Lord our God
who has rescued us from the lake of misery
bring us to the tree of life.
May he who has destroyed the gates of hell
open to us the door of Paradise.

Christ's Resurrection is the first fruits of the future harvest when all
Creation will share his glory, and the God who makes all things new
will bring His creative work to perfection. Our new birth by water
and the Holy Spirit is only the beginning; the work of our creation is
still going on. We must be patient with our imperfections because
God has not finished with us yet! But God does not wait for us to be
perfect before asking us to show His love to others through our lives.
Though we get things wrong, we can still use the talents we have, and
can thank God for what He had already done for us and in us. His
craftsmanship can make something beautiful even out of our faults,
and we can trust Him to bring to completion the work He has begun
in us.

Deus qui, a blessing for the Easter season in the Benedictional of
Archbishop Robert (see p. 20), BR p. 17.

Sixth Sunday of Easter

Year A: *The Spirit of life and love*

> May the Lord, who created all things out of nothing,
> give us his blessing;
> through the Holy Spirit, poured out in our baptism,
> may he grant us forgiveness of all our sins.
>
> He gave the same Holy Spirit to his disciples in tongues of fire;
> through his light may our hearts shine brightly,
> and burn with love for him.
>
> His grace cleanses us from all our faults;
> may his help and guidance keep us safe from all harm,
> and make us to be temples for his indwelling.

In John 14.18 Jesus assures his disciples that he will not leave them desolate like orphans. His going away from them will be for their good, because his coming to them again through the Holy Spirit will make possible a still more intimate relationship with God. Though no longer incarnate beside them, God will then be dwelling within them as the soul of their soul and the ground of their being. It takes us more than a lifetime to explore the riches which were given to us at our baptism, when God's Spirit was poured out upon us. No single English word can express what is meant by calling the Holy Spirit 'the Paraclete': it means Comforter, Strengthener, Encourager, Advocate; someone who is on our side and speaks up for us against the inner voices which tell us we are no good; someone who affirms us as God's children, assured of His love. This prayer asks that the fire of the Holy Spirit will enkindle love in our hearts; that He will help us, guide us, and keep us safe. Jesus assures us in Luke 11.13 that if we human beings know how to give good things to our children, how much more will our heavenly Father give the Holy Spirit to those who ask him.

Benedicat, the blessing for Pentecost week in the Benedictional of Archbishop Robert (see p. 20), BR p. 22.

Sixth Sunday of Easter

Year B: see **Eighth Sunday in Ordinary Time,** *A prayer for fruitfulness,* p. 51.

Year C: *The Spirit: Creator and Encourager*

O fire of the Spirit, the Comforter, life of all living creatures;
in Your holiness You shape and form all things and bring them
    to life.
In Your holiness You give Your healing unction
to those whose fragile lives have been broken;
in Your holiness You tend their infected wounds.

O gentle breath of sanctity, O fire of love;
O taste of sweetness in the heart, and inner fragrance of
    goodness.
O spring of clearest water on which we gaze,
and see that God is gathering together those who are far off,
and is seeking the lost.
O breastplate of life, hope which binds together all the body's
    limbs
and girdles them with goodness, save those whom You have
    blessed.
Watch over those whom the enemy has imprisoned,
and release them from their bonds,
since Your Divine power longs for their salvation.
O strong, safe pathway, stretching everywhere on earth
and reaching every height and depth,
You hold together all things, and bind them into one.
Through You the clouds glide, the breezes fly,
the rocks have their being, the streams flow with water,
and the earth distils its moisture in green growth.
You also guide unfailingly all those
whom Your inbreathed wisdom has instructed and made glad.

Praise be to You, for Yours is the voice which sounds in our
    praising,
and You are the joy of our lives.
As you give us Your shining gifts, Your strength is our hope
    and our glory.

This poem is by HILDEGARD OF BINGEN (1098–1179), who was Abbess of the Benedictine convent of Rupertsberg, near Bingen-am-Rhein.

All the five senses are involved in Hildegard's celebration of the creative and life-giving Spirit of God. As the sound of her words and music filled the convent chapel, the Spirit was audibly inbreathing those praises of God. Some of the images she uses are visual ones, such as fire and water; some are images which can be felt: the breath of sanctity, like a gentle breeze, or the putting-on of a breastplate, making us feel safely enclosed and protected. Julian of Norwich, in fourteenth-century England, was to use a similar image: as our clothes enfold and enclose our bodies, so are we enfolded and enclosed in the goodness of God. (See *Enfolded in Love*, The Julian Shrine, Norwich, 1980, p. 6.) Hildegard also includes the other two senses: the Holy Spirit is a taste of sweetness and a fragrance of goodness. As the Spirit sustains our being, and that of all created things, it is right that our whole selves, with all our senses and powers, should be involved in responding to that life-giving love.

O ignis spiritus, Hildegard's Sequence on the Holy Spirit, AH p. 484.

Hildegard was a visionary and a creation-centred theologian; she wrote about science and medicine, engaged in sharply prophetic correspondence with leading churchmen (including St Bernard), and was an artist, musical composer, and poet of startling originality. Hildegard was very much her own woman: the Sequences which she wrote for the nuns of her Rhineland convent obey none of the usual musical or poetic rules, but her unorthodox methods produced results which are powerful, prayerful, and beautiful.

Another of her Sequences is translated below in Part II, set for Feasts of Women Saints, and the Latin text and music of her *Columba aspexit* (for St Maximinus) is given in Peter Dronke, *The Medieval Lyric*, (London 1968) pp. 233–35.

Rogationtide

Creation greets the Risen Christ

At his rising all created things greet Christ with joy.
Flowers and cornfields flourish with new fruitfulness;
birds sing their sweet delight, now the sad season of frost is
   past.

Darkened at his death, the sun and moon now shine more
   brightly;
the risen Christ is welcomed by the green earth,
which, at his crucifixion, trembled as if about to fall.

Stars, earth, and sea rejoice,
and all the choirs of blessed spirits in the heavens
thank the Trinity.

So let us too be glad today,
for Jesus, in his rising,
opens up to us the path of life.

NOTKER (see pp. 24–25) alludes to St Matthew's account of the
Crucifixion, where the eclipse (27.45) and the earthquake (27.51)
seem to indicate that the natural world was recoiling in horror at the
death of God's Son. He contrasts this with the new life and fresh green
growth of the earth's springtime: after the death-like sleep of winter
all created things seem to be awaking to welcome the risen Christ.
Perhaps Notker took his inspiration from a poem by Venantius
Fortunatus (540–600) part of which is still often used as an Easter
processional hymn: 'Hail thee, festival day' contains the words 'Every
good gift of the year now with its Master returns'.
   This poem reminds us of the unity of all Creation: at Rogationtide
humanity is at one with the world of nature and with the hosts of
heaven in celebrating the joyful new life of Easter.

Favent igitur, the last section of Notker's Easter Sequence *Laudes
salvatori* (see p. 36), NP p. 28.
   The observance of Rogationtide, when God's blessing is asked on
the growing crops, has a long history. The Greater Litanies on 25th
April (which later became St Mark's Day) are thought to be a
Christianization of the pagan Roman ceremonies called *Robigalia* –
the goddess Robigo was thought to protect the corn from blight. The

Lesser Litanies on the three days before Ascension Day are a legacy of the Gallican church: Bishop Mamertus of Vienne, south of Lyons, ordered processional litanies on these days to ask God's protection against the earthquakes and volcanic eruptions which were troubling the area at that time (c. 450). They appear at Rome in the Gregorian Sacramentary and were made compulsory in England by the Council of Clovesho in 747.

Edmund Bishop has a lively account (in *Liturgica Historica*, Oxford 1918, p. 325) of the Rogation processions about the year 800 at the abbey of St Riquier in Picardy. They included crosses, relics, and banners from the surrounding village churches; everyone walked seven abreast (because of the seven gifts of the Spirit), but the infirm were allowed to ride on horseback. The literate encouraged the illiterate to join in the responses in the Litany of the Saints; the monks from the abbey sang psalms, while the schoolboys, and anyone else who could, sang the three Creeds and the Lord's Prayer.

The same spirit of lively communal liturgy pervaded the Rogation processions in medieval England. In some places a dragon, made to look 'laughing and proud', would be carried at the front on the first day, in the middle on the second, and at the end on the third. This represented Evil being gradually beaten back by the grace of God and the power of prayer. When the procession had reached the furthest point of the parish boundaries, the Gospel for Ascension Day (Mark 16.14ff) was solemnly sung. Local rivalries sometimes surfaced: the Canons of York in the late fourteenth century would not always allow the Benedictines of St Mary's to end their procession in the Minster, so their *Ordinale* carefully specifies an alternative route, just in case! (*The Ordinale of St Mary's Abbey, York*, Vol. 2, Henry Bradshaw Society 1936, p. 318.)

Ascension Day

The triumph of Christ

Today the almighty King ascends in triumph
to the heavens from which he came;
the strength of his victory has redeemed the world.

For forty sacred days after his Resurrection
he made the hearts of the apostles strong with his
    encouragement.
He left them with precious kisses of peace;
he gave them power to forgive sins,
and sent them into the world to baptize each living soul
in the mercy of the Father, of the Son, and Holy Spirit.

As he ate with them,
he told them to wait for the gift he had promised.
'Soon', he said, 'I shall send the Spirit into the world;
he shall be your Encourager,
and you will be my witnesses'.

When he had said this,
he was lifted up before their eyes.
A bright cloud received him,
and, though they gazed into the sky,
they saw him no longer.

This poet catches something of the disciples' wistful longing in the
Ascension story, as Jesus is received into the bright cloud of God's
glory and is lost to their sight. But Jesus does not leave them desolate:
as he had encouraged them with his presence after his Resurrection,
so he promises that the Spirit will continue that encouragement, and
will enable them to minister God's grace and mercy to others, so that
all may finally share Christ's heavenly glory.

Rex omnipotens (selected verses), SM p. 470.
    This Sequence is found in the early tenth-century tropers from the
Limoges region of Aquitaine. It was sung on Ascension Day throughout England and France, and occurs also in Italy, Spain, and Belgium,
though not in Germany. Its melody, called *Cithara* or *Occidentana*,
was used by Notker for his Pentecost Sequence *Sancti Spiritus assit*
(see above, p. 40).

Seventh Sunday of Easter

A prayer at Ascensiontide

May Almighty God bless us at this time
when His only Son entered into the highest heavens
and opened up for us the approaches to heaven,
so that, where he is, we too might ascend.

As he was seen plainly by his disciples after his Resurrection,
so may he grant in his mercy
that we may see him smile graciously upon us
when he comes to be our judge.

We believe that he is enthroned in majesty with the Father;
may we also know the truth of his promise
that he shall remain with us until the end of the world.

The name 'Jesus' is the Latinized Greek form of the Hebrew 'Joshua', and Joshua was the pioneer, the trail-blazer, who led his people into the promised land. So Jesus, our new Joshua, is called in the Epistle to the Hebrews 'the Pioneer of our faith' (12.2); he opens up for us the way to heaven, where he is enthroned at God's right hand, so that we may share his glory. He is our High Priest who has consecrated himself to God for our sakes (John 17.19) so that, in union with him, we might come to that full stature of humanity which God wants for us.

This prayer expresses the paradox of Ascensiontide: Jesus the Pioneer has gone on ahead of us, and yet he is also with us at whatever stage of our life's journey we happen to be. On the mount of the Ascension he assures his disciples 'I am with you always, to the end of time' (Matthew 28.20).

Benedicat, the blessing for Ascension Day in the Benedictional of Archbishop Robert (see p. 20), BR p. 21.

In the manuscript, this blessing is like those for Christmas, Easter, and Pentecost in being written in gold letters within an ornamental border.

Pentecost

Sinai revisited: the fire of love

The heavens are aglow with joy,
all the good things of creation voice their sweet praises,
touched by the wind-blown flame of the Holy Spirit.

It will blow today
on all those whose hearts are undivided
and they shall be filled.

For this day's festival renews
the ancient mysteries revealed
on Sinai's mount to Moses;

O truly deep and blessed joys:
man comes to seek the things above;
God comes to earth in form of fire.

Two living beings are made one,
the earthly with the heavenly,
creating on this day true peace.

At the Jewish Pentecost commemoration was made of the giving of
the Law to Moses at that awesome meeting between God and humanity amid the fires on Mount Sinai (Exodus 19.18). At the first
Christian Pentecost (Acts 2.3) the Creator Spirit, who indwells all
Creation and is the breath of its life, comes to the apostles in the form
of fire. But this is no giving of a law-code: the fire brings warmth,
encouragement, and passion because it is the fire of God's love. It
melts coldness and fear, destroys barriers of language and culture,
heals the divisions which wound our humanity, and continues to
enhance our God-given human nature, enabling us to grow towards
wholeness and freedom.

Almiphona, SM p. 533.
   This Pentecost Sequence is found in the early tenth-century tropers
from the Limoges region of Aquitaine. It was not sung at Winchester,
but it does occur in at least ten English manuscripts: it is in the fourteenth-century missals from Durham and Whitby, and appears in an
appendix in two of the thirteenth-century Sarum manuscripts edited
by J. Wickham Legg in SM. It is set for the Wednesday of Pentecost

Week in a thirteenth-century Gradual from St Denis in Paris. The main Pentecost Sequence in medieval Europe was Notker's *Sancti Spiritus assit* (see p. 40).

Drama, symbolism, and considerable ingenuity were used in the Middle Ages to celebrate the descent of the Spirit, as is illustrated by the custom-book (*c.* 1400) of St Mary's Abbey in York. In the story in Acts 2 the Spirit came at the third hour of the day, so at that time, during the Office of Terce, the great ninth-century hymn *Veni, Creator Spiritus* was sung, asking for the Spirit's sevenfold gifts. As the hymn began, seven candles were lit, seven monks (including the abbot) censed the altar, and a white dove ('either a live one or a model') descended from the roof! (*The Ordinale of St Mary's Abbey, York*, Vol. 2, pp. 332, Henry Bradshaw Society, 1936). Unless the monks knew a way of training doves to fly downwards, they presumably used a model worked by a pulley, like the one used in York Minster at the Easter Vigil, when the Paschal Candle was lit by a dove descending with a lighted taper in its beak. (See A. Macgregor, *Fire and Light in the Western Triduum*, Collegeville 1992, p. 265.)

Ordinary Time

Trinity Sunday

See 'Third Sunday before Lent, Year B', *The life-giving Trinity*, p. 46.

Corpus Christi – Thanksgiving for Holy Communion

(Thursday after Trinity Sunday)

The banquet of delight

In this high festival of joy lies our salvation:
this is the marriage-feast
in which Christ is united with his Church.

Sweet banquet of happiness and delight!
Here the sinful find relief and comfort,
and those without hope are given space to breathe and recover.

Here the faithful receive their rewards,
and the joys of the angels are daily renewed,
as the work of love's grace spreads ever more widely.

Out of his ever-gracious regard for us,
the Fountain of Wisdom ordained this feast
to last through all the ages of this changing world.

May Christ create us anew as we join in his marriage-feast;
may he bring us to share in those true riches
which his saints enjoy at the heavenly banquet.

In the Eucharist Christ gives himself to us as the food which sustains our lives. By sharing this foretaste of the heavenly banquet we are made one with him and with each other. Now, as in his earthly life, Jesus shares his table with sinners: his welcome heals us, and his indwelling delights us. The life of God is under our skins, affirming us and helping us towards abundant life.

O sollempnis, the last section of *Jerusalem et Sion filiae*, SM p. 474.
    This is the first of two Sequences set in the thirteenth-century Sarum manuscripts for the feast of the Dedication of a Church. In

England it occurs also in the Westminster Missal (*c.* 1385) and in the slightly later Sherborne Missal. It was sung by the Victorines in Paris and survived in France into the mid-sixteenth century in printed missals from Paris and Coutances in Normandy. The Parisian writer Clichtoveus also commented on it in his *Elucidarium* of 1517. Kehrein in LS wrongly attributes *Jerusalem et Sion* to Adam of St Victor, but says that it occurs in a twelfth-century manuscript at Colmar, south of Strasbourg, which had belonged to the monastery of Marbach. The piece is one of the many Sequences of varied date and provenance collected in the Codex Brander, a sumptuous commemorative volume made in 1507 for the Abbey of St Gall in Switzerland. Other parts of this Sequence are translated in the *English Hymnal* at no. 172, where its lovely Sarum melody is also given.

Though Votive Masses of the Holy Trinity had been popular since the eighth century (the arrangement of their Propers being attributed to Alcuin of York), the Feast itself was established only gradually, largely under Benedictine influence. With its typical conservatism, Rome resisted this innovation; it declared it a Greater Double Feast in 1334 and a Principal Feast as late as 1499.

The Feast of Corpus Christi, honouring the presence of Christ in the Eucharist, began with a vision granted to Juliana of Cornillon, a Béguine who became an Augustinian nun. It was made a local feast in Liège in 1246, and when Liège's Archdeacon became Pope Urban IV it was extended to the whole of the Western Church in 1264, though it was not observed everywhere until after 1317. Thomas Aquinas composed its Propers, including its magnificent Office Hymns and the Sequence *Lauda Sion* (*English Hymnal* nos. 317, 326, and 330). In the towns and villages of medieval Europe it grew into a celebration involving the whole community: processions would go through the streets, and, in cities such as York, the trade guilds would perform mystery plays which portrayed in vivid contemporary language the whole drama of Creation, Fall, and Redemption.

If the Sunday between 24 and 28 May inclusive follows Trinity Sunday, see 'Eighth Sunday in Ordinary Time', p. 50 (Years A and B) or p. 51 (Year C).

Proper 4 – Ninth Sunday in Ordinary Time

(Sunday between 29 May and 4 June inclusive, if after Trinity Sunday)

Year A: *Founded on God's peace*

> May Almighty God order our days in His peace,
> and grant us the gift of His blessing.
>
> May He set us free from all our anxiety,
> and firmly establish our minds on the foundation of His peace
> and tranquillity.
>
> May He adorn our lives with the jewels of faith, hope, and love;
> may He keep us from all harm in this present world,
> and lead us safely into life everlasting.

If we seek our ultimate security in God's unshakeable love for us, then, whatever life may throw at us, our foundations will be built on rock and not on sand. Advertisers' rhetoric tries to play on our anxieties and insecurities in a bid to persuade us to spend money on their products or services; their assumption is that joy, peace, and abundant life consists in an abundance of money or possessions. This prayer, by contrast, suggests that the real jewels, the truly precious treasures, are faith, hope, and love. 'How hard it will be' says Jesus 'for those who have riches to enter the kingdom of God! (Mark 10. 23). Riches need not be material ones: we can pile up kingdom-shutting riches by cultivating a sense of intellectual or cultural superiority. As Harry Williams says in *The True Wilderness* (London 1965, p. 60) 'The most destructive riches of all are religious riches. How prone we are to trust them. Perhaps it is our sound attitude towards the Bible ... or those warm feelings when we pray'. Only by swallowing our pride and learning to receive can we be truly rich; only then can we know the deep peace and lasting joy that God wants for us.

Omnipotens Deus dies, the blessing for the 21st Sunday after Pentecost in the Benedictional of Archbishop Robert (see p. 20), BR p. 28.

Proper 4 – Ninth Sunday in Ordinary Time

(Sunday between 29 May and 4 June inclusive, if after Trinity Sunday)

Year B: *The freedom of Grace*

> Flowers bloom on Aaron's rod,
> a maiden bears the Son of God –
> miracle of virgin birth;
> this new child is our new brother,
> this young girl is our new mother;
> wondrous newness: God on earth.
>
> Rub the corn-ear, pluck the grain,
> trust yourself to Truth, and gain
> freedom from your bondage sore.
> Lift the veil from Moses' face;
> heaven's clouds, which rain down Grace,
> melt the winter of the Law.

'You are not under the Law, but under Grace' says St Paul (Romans 6.14), and in the Epistle to the Hebrews (9.15) Jesus is called 'the mediator of a new covenant', a new relationship between God and His people, which began when His Son was born at Bethlehem into a human family. The radical newness of the Incarnation means that the whole family of humanity is now God's family; Jesus calls us his brothers and sisters. This means that we can enjoy 'the glorious liberty of the children of God' (Romans 8.21). Our new relationship with God is based on intimacy and trust, not on keeping rules, as Jesus shows when he plucks the ears of corn on the Sabbath (Mark 2.23). St Paul in 2 Corinthians 3.12ff expressed this intimacy through the image of the removal of the veil with which Moses covered his face after he had spoken with God (Exodus 34.34); in Jesus we see God and can speak with Him face to face. This poet adds his own image, based on Isaiah 45.8, of the winter of the old Law being melted by the fresh spring rains of God's Grace.

Virga floret, part of *Ecce sonat in aperto*, SM p. 495.
    This appears to be an English Sequence, confined to the Sarum Use. It is in two of the thirteenth-century manuscripts edited by Wickham Legg in SM: the 'Crawford Missal' from the diocese of Exeter, and the Bologna manuscript from Oxford. The Sequences are collected together at the end of these manuscripts, and the collection ends with

a serious of eighteen Marian pieces, of which *Ecce sonat* is the seventeenth. Its style suggests a late twelfth- or early thirteenth-century date.

Proper 4 – Ninth Sunday in Ordinary Time

(Sunday between 29 May and 4 June inclusive, if after Trinity Sunday)

Year C: see 'Fourth Sunday before Lent, Year B', *Christ our healer*, p. 41.

Proper 5 – Tenth Sunday in Ordinary Time

(Sunday between 5 and 11 June inclusive, if after Trinity Sunday)

Year A: *The call of Matthew*

Our heart and our flesh rejoice in God,
for, when Christ Jesus called Matthew to himself,
the lowly sparrow found itself a home:
Matthew left the fetters of his worldly cares behind him,
and his heart flew up on high.

Now and for ever let us praise the Father of mercies for His
    goodness,
for He has placed the converted publican among His apostles
    and evangelists.
He who once transgressed the law now preaches the gospel;
such is the fruit of penitence, and of grace shown to the fallen.

All the debts owed by this servant have been cancelled by God;
taught by this example,
he knows that he too should have mercy on his fellow-servants.

As we believe that Christ made Matthew whole,
so may he also heal the wounds of all our sins.

GOTTSCHALK makes imaginative use of Psalm 84 to express
Matthew's joy at being called into fellowship with Jesus. There he
finds himself accepted, cherished, and truly at home; his heart flies
upwards like the sparrow finding its nest in the house of God. We too
can rejoice in God, because His Son welcomes us to his table, despite
our sins. Our true home is being in his presence, where we are
affirmed and made whole by his limitless love.

Selected verses from the Sequence *In Deum exultet*, LS p. 307.
    Gottschalk (see pp. 107–108) loved to weave psalm-texts into his
Sequences. Another example is his *Caeli enarrant* for Apostles, based
on Psalm 19 (see p. 106).
    In Deum only achieved a limited circulation; the text in LS comes
from a twelfth-century Gratz manuscript. Most churches on St
Matthew's Day used the Sequence for the Common of Apostles, *Clare
sanctorum* by Notker. An exception was Whitby, where in the fourteenth century the monks sang the 'Publican's Lament', *Stans a longe*

(translated below under 'Proper 25, Year C', and in *Paths of the Heart*, p. 56).

Proper 5 – Tenth Sunday in Ordinary Time

(Sunday between 5 and 11 June inclusive, if after Trinity Sunday)

Year B: *Sharing the life of God*

> May the Lord pour down upon us
> the gentle rain of his blessings,
> and open to us the heavenly treasures of his glory.
>
> May the Lord make us sharers in his eternal life,
> and heirs of the kingdom of heaven.
>
> May the Holy Spirit find in us
> a dwelling-place fit for Himself,
> and may His glorious majesty
> be pleased to rest within our hearts.

Anyone who does God's will is called by Jesus his brother, or sister, or mother (Mark 3.35). As members of his family, we are promised a share in his eternal life, where the weight of glory prepared for us by God is out of all proportion to the troubles which weigh us down here (2 Corinthians 4.17). The God of all consolation comforts us in all our troubles through the indwelling of the Holy Spirit, who brings to our minds Christ's words of eternal life, a source of living strength to all who believe (2 Corinthians 1.3f; John 6.68; 1 Thessalonians 2.13).

Benedictionum, the blessing for the Sunday after the Ascension in the Benedictional of Archbishop Robert (see p. 20), BR p. 21.

Proper 5 – Tenth Sunday in Ordinary Time

(Sunday between 5 and 11 June inclusive, if after Trinity Sunday)

Year C: *Christ our Resurrection*

'I am Alpha and Omega, the First and the Last,
the Beginning and the End.
I was alive before the world began,
I live throughout all ages, without end.

My hands, which made you, were pierced through by nails;
for your sakes I was whipped, and crowned with thorns.
I asked for water on the Cross,
they offered vinegar to drink;
they gave me gall to eat,
and thrust a spear into my side.
I died, and was buried.

But I am risen and am still with you;
see that it is I myself – there is no God apart from me.
I am your Redemption, I am your King,
and I will raise you up on the last day.
Alleluia!'

Those who saw Jesus raise to life Jairus' daughter and the widow's son at Nain were naturally filled with awe and amazement (Mark 5.42; Luke 7.16). Restoring the dead to life is a Divine prerogative, and this is made more explicit in St John's Gospel, where Jesus says 'I am the resurrection and the life' (11.25). In this poem the glorified Christ begins and ends his discourse with more 'I am' sayings, drawn from the poet's imagination as he meditates on scripture (e.g. Revelation 1). But they are the framework for a moving memorial of the Passion: Jesus shows that God is in loving solidarity with His human creatures; He shares our suffering, as we will share His glory.

Ego sum alpha, an Antiphon before the Gospel sung on Easter Sunday in the thirteenth century at Chartres Cathedral. The Latin text is given by David Hiley in an article about a Chartres manuscript Gradual containing Tropes and Sequences, 'Provins, Bibliothèque Municipale 12 (24)', in W. Arlt and G. Björkvall (eds.), *Recherches nouvelles sur les Tropes Liturgiques* (Stockholm 1993) p. 251).

Antiphonae ante Evangelium were sung during the Gospel procession, and begun after the singing of the Sequence had ended. Probably a survival from the ancient Gallican rite, they occur at several places in France (including the Abbey of St Denis in Paris as well as at Chartres) on just three occasions in the year, Christmas, Epiphany, and Easter. They are also a feature of the Ambrosian liturgy at Milan.

Proper 6 – Eleventh Sunday in Ordinary Time

(Sunday between 12 and 18 June inclusive, if after Trinity Sunday)

Year A: *The calling of the Twelve*

Those things which seem foolish and weak in the eyes of the
world
have been raised up by God and exalted to places of honour.
These men were chosen by God, and were filled with the power
to bear faithful witness to Him and His truth in the world.

Like the skies, the apostles contain celestial secrets;
like the clouds, they send forth the gentle rain of sound
doctrine.
They are the temple's foundations, its courts and fair portals;
pillars of strength on which the Church is established.

Through their words and their deeds God's light shines forth in
the world;
salt of the earth, they season our lives with their wisdom.
They are our shepherds, who tend all the sheep in their care;
they are our teachers, directing our minds to the truth.

Let us then ask for their prayerful support and assistance,
so that with them we may share heaven's joys in our homeland.

Before the apostles were sent out to bear witness to God's love in the
world and to be the shepherds of His people, their calling was simply
to be in Jesus' presence and to learn from him. We too need to receive
the love of Christ in prayer and sacrament if we are to show it to
others. We are called, as they were, to let the light of God's love shine
out through us, and to be like salt, bringing out life's true flavour. The
image of the apostles as foundation-stones of the new Jerusalem
comes from Revelation 21.14, and the comparing of them to skies and
clouds is an allusion to Psalm 19 'The heavens declare the glory of
God'; its verse 'Their sound is gone out into all lands, and their words
unto the ends of the world' was often applied to the apostles.

Stulta quoque, the last part of *Cuius laus*, a Sequence for feasts of
apostles found in a fourteenth-century manuscript from
Donaueschingen and in a sixteenth-century printed missal from
Poitiers, LS p. 269.

Psalm 19.4 ('Their sound is gone out ...') was the Gradual verse, sung just before the Sequence, in Masses of the Apostles, so medieval poets naturally thought of the apostles as being like the heavens which declared the glory of God. *Cuius laus* contains a phrase ('*Hi sunt caeli*') which is a quotation from a better-known Sequence on the same theme, the eleventh-century *Caeli enarrant*, attributed to Gottschalk of Aachen. This was common in Germany and (unlike *Cuius laus*) appears in England at York and Whitby. Part of it is translated in *Paths of the Heart* (London 1993) p. 90. The sky- and cloud-imagery was still being used in the seventeenth century: it occurs in the hymn translated as 'Disposer supreme' (*English Hymnal* no. 178).

Proper 6 – Eleventh Sunday in Ordinary Time

(Sunday between 12 and 18 June inclusive, if after Trinity Sunday)

Year B: see 'Fourth Sunday of Epiphany, Year B', *Christ our teacher*, p. 32.

Year C: *The woman at the banquet*

> She embraces the Lord's feet,
> she washes them with tears,
> she wipes them with her hair.
>
> Washing them,
> wiping them,
> she anoints them with ointment,
> she circles them with kisses.
>
> These are the banquets
> in which you take delight,
> O Wisdom of the Father;
>
> born of a virgin,
> you thought it not beneath you
> to be touched by a sinner.
>
> A Pharisee invited you,
> but that which Mary offered
> satisfied you.

Tradition identifies the woman at the banquet in Luke 7.36 with Mary Magdalen. Martin Thornton in *The Purple-headed Mountain* (London 1962) points out that her penitence, her openness to receive God's forgiveness, did not mean a suppression of the passionate impulses of her nature, but rather their re-direction: 'She simply stopped loving the wrong things and began to love God' (p. 85).

Pedes amplectitur from the Sequence *Laus tibi Christe* by GOTTSCHALK OF AACHEN, YM p. 66. (This translation first appeared in *Paths of the Heart* (London 1993) p. 82.)

Gottschalk (*c.* 1010–98) was a monk of Limburg who became Provost of Aachen and court chaplain. He dedicated a book of Sequences to the Emperor Henry IV. He wrote in the tradition of

Notker, and, though his use of imagery could sometimes be bizarre, he was capable, as in this piece, of writing vividly and with tenderness. See F. J. E. Raby, *A History of Christian-Latin Poetry* (2nd Edition, Oxford 953), pp. 224ff.

Laus tibi Christe was sung on St Mary Magdalen's Day in Germany, for example by the Cistercians of Kaisheim, and in England at Canterbury, York, and Durham. The Sarum books follow the French tradition of singing *Mane prima sabbati* on that day. (*Mane prima* is translated below in Part II under '22 July'.)

Proper 7 – Twelfth Sunday in Ordinary Time

(Sunday between 19 and 25 June inclusive, if after Trinity Sunday)

Year A: see 'Second Sunday of Epiphany, Year B', *Following God's way*, p. 26.

Year B: see 'Fifth Sunday before Lent, Year B', *Signs of Godhead*, p. 36.

Proper 7, Year C: as Year B.

Twelfth Sunday in Ordinary Time, Year C: see 'Third Sunday before Lent, Year A', *Christ our life*, p. 44.

Proper 8 – Thirteenth Sunday in Ordinary Time

(Sunday between 26 June and 2 July inclusive)

Year A: see 'Third Sunday before Lent, Year A', *Christ our life*, p. 44.

Year B: see 'Proper 5, Year C', *Christ our Resurrection*, p. 103.

Year C: see 'Second Sunday of Epiphany, Year B', *Following God's way*, p. 26.

Proper 9 – Fourteenth Sunday in Ordinary Time

(Sunday between 3 and 9 July inclusive)

Year A: see 'Fourth Sunday before Lent, Year C', *The fountain of life*, p. 42.

Year B: *The Spirit's inbreathing*

> O Lord, king of boundless goodness,
> listen to the devout praises of Your servants;
> You sent Your own Son from heaven
> to save a lost world,
> have mercy upon us.
>
> O Christ, by the gracious breathing of the Spirit
> you were born of the Virgin Mary
> and became man for humankind,
> have mercy upon us.
>
> O Holy Spirit, proceeding from the Father and the Son,
> sent to us from them, and one in substance with them,
> co-equal and co-eternal;
> You inspired the prophets to speak in many different ways
> of the mysteries of heavenly glory;
> pour Your gifts into our hearts,
> and have mercy upon us.

Prophets may sometimes be 'fore-tellers', but primarily they are 'forth-tellers', boldly speaking the truth even when this arouses strong opposition, as happened to Jesus when he preached on his home territory (Mark 6.4; Luke 4.28–9). We affirm in the Creed that the Holy Spirit speaks through the message of the prophets – and prophets are needed in every generation. We need the inbreathed wisdom of the Spirit to aid us in the difficult task of facing up to uncomfortable truths ourselves and helping others to do the same.

Part of *Rex immensae*, a Trope (see p. 47) to the *Kyrie* found in the York and Hereford Missals, YM p. 247.

As with most *Kyrie*-tropes, this one is in Trinitarian form, the second set of Kyries being addressed to the Holy Spirit.

Tropes as a *genre* have the distinction of being the seed-bed from which sprang the whole exuberant growth of modern European drama. A Trope in dialogue form was sung in many churches from the tenth century onwards as an introduction to the Introit chant at Mass on Easter Day. A monk in a white alb would conceal himself by the Easter Sepulchre (where the Blessed Sacrament had been reserved since Maundy Thursday) and would play the part of the angel at the tomb. The women with their spices were represented by three monks who approached the sepulchre bearing thuribles with incense. The angel asked them 'Whom do you seek in the sepulchre, O worshippers of Christ?' and the women replied 'Jesus of Nazareth who was crucified, O heavenly one'. As the dialogue led into the Introit 'I am risen', the Sacrament was brought in triumph from the tomb to the altar. With this *Quem quaeritis* Trope the drama of the liturgy became liturgical drama: other playlets developed from it, and were performed at various feasts in the Church's year. (There was a Christmas version of *Quem quaeritis* in which the shepherds were asked 'Whom do you seek in the manger?') Later, the drama moved outside the church building in the form of the miracle and mystery plays which were the parents of modern secular drama. For more details see O. B. Hardison, *Christian Rite and Christian Drama in the Middle Ages* (Baltimore 1965).

In the later Middle Ages at Durham Cathedral, when the Sacrament was brought to the High Altar on Easter morning, a monstrance was used in the form of a statue of Christ containing a crystal, through which the Host could be seen. The procession is described in R. W. J. Austin, *The Rites of Durham* (Durham, n.d.) p. 44.

Proper 9 – Fourteenth Sunday in Ordinary Time

(Sunday between 3 and 9 July inclusive)

Year C: *Christ our peace*

> Your lips, O God, have given us Your promise
> that You will give peace to all people,
> and You have left us Your teachings
> which make for peace.
>
> Pour into our minds an eager desire for peace and goodwill;
> cleanse us from the stain of all our sins;
> may we seek peace by our words and our actions,
> and hold it fast in purity of heart.
>
> May the peace, faith, and love
> of our Lord Jesus Christ and all the saints
> be with us, and remain with us always.

For the New Testament writers, peace meant much more than simply an absence of hostility. It was a word charged with all the blessedness of being in a right relationship with God, other people, and oneself. St James sees it (3.17) as a characteristic of that heavenly wisdom which comes to us as a free and undeserved gift from God – a gift which Christ has made it possible for us to receive. Appropriating the gift means accepting God's acceptance of us, His delight in us as we are, and His belief in what we can become. The peace and joy of knowing how much God values us already take away the need for jealous jockeying for position: in Mark 9.36 Jesus sets a child in the midst of his quarrelling disciples to teach them to accept themselves and their lives as a gift from God's hands. The riches of being loved by God mean that we can afford to delight in His gifts to others, and thus become peacemakers, sowing seeds of peace that will yield a harvest of joy (James 3.18). As the seventy disciples found (Luke 10.5) the gift of peace multiplies as it is shared with others.

Deus per cuius, a prayer at the Kiss of Peace from the sixth Sunday Mass in the *Missale Gothicum* (see p. 26), MG p. 139.

When it was used liturgically in seventh- or eighth-century Gaul, the last sentence of this prayer was sung: it is written in the margin of the manuscript with an early form of musical notation.

Proper 10 – Fifteenth Sunday in Ordinary Time

(Sunday between 10 and 16 July inclusive)

Year A: see 'Fourth Sunday of Epiphany, Year B', *Christ our teacher*, p. 32.

Year B: see 'Fifth Sunday of Easter, Year C', *Christ who creates us anew* p. 85.

Year C: *Loving God and our neighbour*

> May the Lord grant us the gift of His blessing
> and fill us with the Spirit of truth and peace.
> May we walk with faithful hearts
> along the way of salvation,
> and avoid the lurking snares of sin.
>
> May our devotion to God be shown forth in our lives
> through sincere love for our neighbour,
> so that we may come in safety to the kingdom of heaven.

This prayer reminds us that the commandment to love God with all our heart is inseparable from the commandment to love our neighbour as ourselves (Matthew 22.37; Mark 12.29). We often overlook the fact that these commandments involve not a two-fold love, but a three-fold one: we shall not be able to love God or our neighbour unless we can also love ourselves, because God loves us. Before we can follow the example of the Good Samaritan (Luke 10.25ff) and 'go and do likewise', we must recognize that we are often in the position of the man in the ditch: we need to receive the loving ministrations of the Good Samaritan who is Christ – a despised figure who does not shrink from getting involved in our messiness, and who heals us at great cost to himself. Inner wounds take time to heal: we go on needing the soothing oil and the astringent wine, the 'rough and holy love' which is making us whole. Knowing our need helps us to notice (unlike Dives in Luke 16.19ff) those on our doorsteps who are in pain and need, and to share with them some of the love we have received from God.

Det vobis Dominus, a blessing from the Benedictional of Archbishop Robert (see p. 20), BR p. 26.

The phrase 'rough and holy love' comes from a short story, 'A Pilgrimage to the Dark', by Caroline Glyn in *A Mountain at the End of Night* (London 1977), p. 54.

Proper 11 – Sixteenth Sunday in Ordinary Time

(Sunday between 17 and 23 July inclusive)

Year A: see 'Eighth Sunday in Ordinary Time, Year C', *A prayer for fruitfulness*, p. 51.

Year B: see 'Fourth Sunday of Easter', *The Good Shepherd*, p. 82.

Year C: *Mutual love and peace*

> O Lord and Creator of all things,
> You are always present with Your creatures in graciousness
>   and love.
> Lazarus, restored to life, relaxed with You in his home;
> Martha busily served You; Mary washed Your feet;
> the whole house was filled with love.
>
> Grant that Your people may so love one another,
> that they may be united in Your peace.
> As Mary's tears flowed from her great love,
> so may we too sorrow for our sins;
> may our prayer be as fragrant as the precious ointment
> which she poured over Your sacred feet;
> and so let us offer one another our kiss of peace,
> as Mary kissed the feet of her Redeemer,
> the Saviour of the world.

The author of this prayer from seventh-century Gaul evokes the atmosphere of love and peace which filled the house at Bethany like the fragrance of Mary's ointment. The tension between the sisters in Luke 10.40 has been resolved: as in John 12.3, the two women express their love for Jesus in ways which accord with their different temperaments; the tears of penitence come from Luke 7.38. Christ's loving acceptance of Martha, Mary, and Lazarus brings reconciliation: it enables difference to be celebrated and rejoiced in, rather than resented.

Universorum ipse, from the *Missale Gothicum* (see p. 26), MG p. 61.
    The prayer is a *Collectio ad Pacem*, a prayer which preceded the exchanging of the Kiss of Peace. In the Gallican Rite each Mass had its own variable Prayer at the Peace; this one is set for Palm Sunday,

the day when the Creed was taught to the candidates for Baptism. A *Collectio ad Pacem* for an ordinary Sunday is translated above on p. 112.

Proper 12 – Seventeenth Sunday in Ordinary Time

(Sunday between 24 and 30 July inclusive)

Year A: *Precious treasure*

> From the humble dust of the earth, O Christ,
> you choose precious jewels,
> and set them in the splendid realms of angelic light.
>
> They are the wonder of those high golden kingdoms
> and a source of sweet devotion to those on earth.
>
> What a noble fortune you spent, O God,
> on the altar of the cross,
> so that your Godhead alone might possess
> these beautiful precious gems,
> whose purity is your loving kindness,
> whose dignity is the glory of heaven.
>
> Praise to you, O Christ our King;
> grant us the crown of your merciful love.

Being gems of doctrine, Christ's parables can be turned this way and that, to catch the light from various angles, and so reveal different facets of the truth and beauty of God. From one point of view, the hidden treasure and the precious pearl in Matthew 13.44f are images of the Kingdom of God. But we can also turn the parable round and, like this poet, dare to see ourselves as jewels which God longed for so much that he spent all His riches on the Cross in order to possess them. He has made us His own: we have been bought at a great price, but it is we who are the partakers of heavenly treasure.

Qui humili from *Cantent te*, YM p. 301. (This translation first appeared in *Paths of the Heart* (London 1993), p. 80.)

   Cantent te is a Sequence for the Feast of St Benedict, probably written at Winchester (see p. 64) in the tenth century and not known elsewhere. It is set in the Winchester Troper to the melody *Ecce quam bonum*, which is the tune of *Laudum carmina*, the usual Sequence for St Benedict in England and France.

Proper 12 – Seventeenth Sunday in Ordinary Time

(Sunday between 24 and 30 July inclusive)

Year B: *Bread from Heaven*

> With joyful hearts let us praise our God,
> who always renews His Church
> when she falls short through her sins.
>
> When she is weak and pale,
> He brightens and warms her
> with the rays of the true sun.
>
> He has led her out of the land of slavery
> with its fiery furnaces;
> when she cries to Him in any kind of distress,
> He hears her.
>
> He nourishes her with bread from heaven,
> and teaches her to love and worship Him.
> With sweet honey from the rock
> He satisfies her.

The stories of Jesus' feeding of the multitudes in a desolate place (John 6.5ff; Matthew 14.15ff) are resonant with echoes of the miraculous feeding of the people of Israel with heavenly manna (Exodus 16.14ff). God had rescued them from slavery in Egypt and was teaching them during their wanderings in the wilderness to rely on His loving care. The feeding-stories also contain eucharistic overtones: Jesus takes, blesses, breaks, and gives the bread, as he was to do at the Last Supper. NOTKER'S poem, with its allusions to Psalm 81, suggests that Jesus is himself the 'bread from heaven' and the 'honey from the rock' with which God feeds and delights His people.

Laeta mente, Notker's Sequence for the Fourth Sunday of Easter in his *Liber Hymnorum* (see pp. 24–25), NP p. 46.
   The title of its melody is *Exultate Deo*, the opening words of Psalm 81, on which the piece is based. It occurs, as might be expected, in chant-books from Notker's abbey of St Gall, in the eleventh-century Prüm Troper, and in a few Italian manuscripts. It does not seem to have survived into the late medieval repertoire. The melody was

known, though set to different words, in tenth-century Aquitaine; unusually for a Sequence-melody, it does not contain any repetition. It´is given in Anselm Hughes, *Anglo-French Sequelae* (Farnborough 1966), p. 41.

Proper 12 – Seventeenth Sunday in Ordinary Time

(Sunday between 24 and 30 July inclusive)

Year C: see 'Sixth Sunday of Easter, Year A' *The Spirit of life and love* p. 86.

Proper 13 – Eighteenth Sunday in Ordinary Time

(Sunday between 31 July and 6 August inclusive)

Year A: see 'Proper 12, Year B', *Bread from Heaven*, p. 117.

Year B: *Bread of life*

> O sweetest Bread, O Christ our life,
> refreshing souls who trust in You;
> O Paschal Victim, meekest Lamb,
> pure offering, and oblation true.
>
> In form of bread You come to us,
> concealing Your divinity;
> You nourish us with gifts of grace
> in all their rich variety.
>
> Your sevenfold Spirit's healing power
> restores and recreates our soul;
> You pledge Your pardon for our sins
> by this great gift which makes us whole.
>
> May we receive You worthily,
> and hold You close within our heart;
> grant, through this earthly food, that we
> at heaven's feast may take our part.

Jesus is the Bread of Life who came down from heaven to give life to the world (John 6.33). In the Eucharist he offers us in union with himself to the Father and gives himself to us to be the food that renews and sustains our lives.

Selected verses from *O Panis dulcissime*, a Sequence for Corpus Christi, LS p. 128.

This Sequence is found in a thirteenth-century St Gall manuscript and became fairly widespread in Switzerland and South Germany in the later Middle Ages. It occurs, for example, at Reichenau in the fourteenth century and at Basel in the sixteenth. The usual Sequence for Corpus Christi is of course St Thomas Aquinas' *Lauda Sion* (see p. 96).

Proper 13 – Eighteenth Sunday in Ordinary Time

(Sunday between 31 July and 6 August inclusive)

Year C: see 'Third Sunday before Lent, Year B', *The life-giving Trinity*, p. 46.

Proper 14 – Nineteenth Sunday in Ordinary Time

(Sunday between 7 and 13 August inclusive)

Year A: see 'Fifth Sunday before Lent, Year B', *Signs of Godhead*, p. 36.

Year B: *Foretaste of Heaven*

> O Lord, mighty maker of all Your creatures,
> be our protector always.
>
> O Christ, you recreate those who share in your Supper
> through the bread which you make to be your Body,
> and you give your people a pledge of their final perfection;
> O Christ, bread from heaven,
> sweet honeycomb, food of eternity,
> whom the orders of angels praise,
> be close to us in our penitence.
>
> O Holy Spirit, Giver of Your seven-fold gifts of grace,
> Consoler of grieving spirits,
> grant that we may truly love You.

'No one can come to me', says Jesus in John 6.44, 'unless the Father draw him'. We come to him because we are drawn by the attractiveness of his merciful love. We come to him because he first comes to us where we are, and accepts us as we are. As we share in his Supper, he fills our lives with his grace, and gives us a pledge of the glory to come, which exceeds all that we can desire.

Part of the *Kyrie*-Trope *Rex immensae*, from the York and Hereford Missals, YM p. 247.
    The rest of this Trope is translated above on p. 110.

Proper 14 – Nineteenth Sunday in Ordinary Time

(Sunday between 7 and 13 August inclusive)

Year C: see 'Fourth Sunday before Lent, Year A' *A prayer for God's Grace* p. 40.

Proper 15 – Twentieth Sunday in Ordinary Time

(Sunday between 14 and 20 August inclusive)

Year A: see 'Third Sunday before Lent, Year B', *The life-giving Trinity*, p. 46.

Year B: *The joy of Christ's presence*

> Hail, most holy Body of Christ!
> You are sweetness and delight to us,
> more than all things that are or ever shall be.
> May the Body of our Lord Jesus Christ
> be to us sinners our Way and our Life.
>
> Hail, wine of heaven!
> You are sweetness and delight to us,
> more than all things that are or ever shall be.
>
> May the Body and Blood of our Lord Jesus Christ
> be an unfailing remedy for us in our sinfulness,
> and lead us to life everlasting.

In the last sermon he preached, Austin Farrer said 'You know what is the special mercy of Christ to us in the Sacraments. It is, that he just puts himself there.' We may not feel 'sweetness and delight' when we receive Communion – we may not feel anything much at all – but, says Jesus, 'Whoever eats my flesh and drinks my blood dwells in me, and I in them' (John 6.56). Beneath our surface feelings, or lack of them, is the deep joy of that mutual indwelling in love.

Ave in eternum, SM p. 227.

In the Sarum Missal, these were the prayers (originally in the first person) said by the priest before he made his Communion. The ancestry of such private devotions lies in the Gallican rite (see p. 26–27), where they could often be highly emotive and verbose. The introduction of the Roman Rite into northern Europe in the eighth century did not lead to their extinction, but it did have a healthy effect in pruning their wordiness and giving a clearer and more restrained expression to their feeling.

The quotation from Austin Farrer comes from his sermon 'Walking Sacraments' in *A Celebration of Faith* (London 1970), p. 109.

Proper 15 – Twentieth Sunday in Ordinary Time

(Sunday between 14 and 20 August inclusive)

Year C: see 'Second Sunday of Epiphany, Year B', *Following God's way*, p. 26.

Proper 16 – Twenty-First Sunday in Ordinary Time

(Sunday between 21 and 27 August inclusive)

Year A: see 'Third Sunday of Epiphany, Year A', *Light of the world*, p. 30.

Year B: see 'Proper 5, Year B', *Sharing the life of God*, p. 102.

Proper 16 Year C: see 'Fifth Sunday before Lent, Year B', *Signs of Godhead*, p. 36.

Twenty-First Sunday in Ordinary Time

Year C: see 'Proper 9, Year C', *Christ our peace* p. 112

Proper 17 – Twenty-Second Sunday in Ordinary Time

(Sunday between 28 August and 3 September inclusive)

Year A: see 'Second Sunday of Epiphany, Year B', *Following God's way*, p. 26.

Year B: see 'Fourth Sunday of Epiphany, Year B', *Christ our teacher*, p. 32.

Year C: see 'Third Sunday before Lent, Year A', *Christ our life*, p. 44.

Proper 18 – Twenty-Third Sunday in Ordinary Time

(Sunday between 4 and 10 September inclusive)

Year A: see 'Proper 10, Year C', *Loving God and our neighbour*, p. 113.

Year B: see 'Fifth Sunday before Lent, Year B', *Signs of Godhead*, p. 36.

Year C: see 'Proper 4, Year A', *Founded on God's peace*, p. 97.

Proper 19 – Twenty-Fourth Sunday in Ordinary Time

(Sunday between 11 and 17 September inclusive)

Year A: see 'Third Sunday before Lent, Year B', *The life-giving Trinity*, p. 46.

Year B: see 'Second Sunday of Epiphany, Year B', *Following God's way*, p. 26.

Year C: *The God who seeks the lost*

> He who created all things in His wisdom
> has helped to regain what our primal foolishness lost:
> our closeness to God,
> lost to us by the serpent,
> and restored to us by a woman.
>
> Like the woman searching the house
> with a brittle potsherd and a kindled lamp,
> You appear in humility to recover the lost coin
> and restore the shining royal image in the human soul.
>
> Let us then sing the song of the angels,
> praising the King of glory and justice,
> who sent to us His only Son,
> that today He might free us from misery
> and grant us the grace of His merciful love.

GUY OF BAZOCHES (d. 1203) was a man of action; he was a hunting, hawking, and fishing clergyman, a Canon of Châlons, who went on the Second Crusade in 1190. In contrast to this 'macho' lifestyle, his image of God's saving love in the Incarnation comes from the domestic world of Jesus' parable of the lost coin in Luke 15.8. We are the coin, and God is the woman on her hands and knees, patiently scraping away with a piece of broken pot among the dust and debris on the floor, searching for the coin. When she finds it, she wipes off the dust, and restores it to its former glory.

Selected verses from *Qui cuncta condidit*, a poem about the Nativity, in F. J. E. Raby, *A History of Christian-Latin Poetry*, Second Edition, (Oxford 1953), p. 308. This translation first appeared in *Paths of the Heart* (London 1993), p. 60.

Guy wrote some quantitative verse in classical elegiacs, but this piece is rhythmical, in a metre well adapted for singing. He composed songs, hymns, and Sequences for various festivals and saints' days, including St Thomas of Canterbury. His Sequences are in the style of the Victorines (see pp. 12 and 16); they are rhythmical and have two-syllabled rhyme.

Proper 20 – Twenty-Fifth Sunday in Ordinary Time

(Sunday between 18 and 24 September inclusive)

Year A: see 'Eighth Sunday in Ordinary Time, Year C', *A prayer for fruitfulness*, p. 51.

Year B: see 'Proper 9, Year C', *Christ our peace*, p. 112.

Year C: see 'Fourth Sunday before Lent, Year A' *A prayer for God's Grace* p. 40.

Proper 21 – Twenty-Sixth Sunday in Ordinary Time

(Sunday between 25 September and 1 October inclusive)

Year A: see 'Fifth Sunday of Lent', *The altar of the Cross*, p. 63.

Year B: see 'Proper 9, Year B', *The Spirit's inbreathing*, p. 110.

Year C: see 'Proper 10, Year C', *Loving God and our neighbour*, p. 113.

Proper 22 – Twenty-Seventh Sunday in Ordinary Time

(Sunday between 2 and 8 October inclusive)

Year A: see 'Fifth Sunday of Easter, Year B', *The True Vine*, p. 83.

Year B: see 'Proper 4, Year B', *The freedom of Grace*, p. 98.

Year C: see 'Fourth Sunday of Epiphany, Year B', *Christ our teacher*, p. 32.

Proper 23 – Twenty-Eighth Sunday in Ordinary Time

(Sunday between 9 and 15 October inclusive)

Year A: see 'Eighth Sunday in Ordinary Time, Year B', *The spiritual marriage*, p. 50.

Year B: see 'Proper 4, Year A', *Founded on God's peace*, p. 97.

Year C: see 'Fifth Sunday of Easter, Year C', *Christ who creates us anew* p. 85.

Proper 24 – Twenty-Ninth Sunday in Ordinary Time

(Sunday between 16 and 22 October inclusive)
Year A: see 'Third Sunday before Lent, Year A', *Christ our life*, p. 44.

Year B: see 'Good Friday', *Conqueror of death*, p. 70.

Year C: *Persevering in trust*

> God knows and understands our human weakness;
> may He grant us the gift of His blessing.
>
> He has given us the desire to seek Him by love and prayer;
> may He also give us His help and comfort.
>
> Through our faith in Him,
> may He sustain us in this life
> and in the life to come;
> for He created us in His goodness,
> and our life is the gift of His love.

In the parable of the Unjust Judge (Luke 18.1–8), Jesus teaches us, with his typically ironic humour, the lesson of perseverance in prayer. We may wonder sometimes if prayers of asking have any point to them at all – after all, does not God 'know our necessities before we ask'? If we are tempted to be more sophisticated than Jesus (who both taught and practised such prayer), we might reflect that petitionary prayer benefits us in two ways: it reminds us that we are not self-sufficient, and it makes us clarify in our minds what it is that we truly and deeply want – which may turn out not to be what we originally prayed for. Jesus' prayer in Gethsemane gives us the pattern: he began by praying the naturally human prayer to be spared death; after wrestling with the question of what God's will for him might be, he ended with an act of trust and self-surrender. Perseverance in prayer leads to a deepening of our trust in God's love for us, whatever happens.

Concedat, a blessing for the Fifteenth Sunday after Pentecost in the Benedictional of Archbishop Robert (see p. 20), BR p. 26.

Proper 25 – Thirtieth Sunday in Ordinary Time

(Sunday between 23 and 29 October inclusive)

Year A: see 'Proper 10, Year C', *Loving God and our neighbour*, p.113.

Year B: see 'Fifth Sunday before Lent, Year B', *Signs of Godhead*, p. 36.

Year C: *The Publican in the Temple*

> Standing afar off
> was a man who had committed many crimes,
> and his troubled mind was dwelling on his sins.
>
> He would not raise his eyes
> towards the high starry heaven
> but, beating his breast, he said these words,
> his face full of tears:
> 'God be merciful to me, a sinner,
> and in Your goodness wipe out my misdeeds.'
>
> These words won for him pity and kindness
> and he went to his house a righteous man.
>
> Let us follow his holy example and say to God:
> 'Merciful God, be gentle with us and free us from sin;
> in Your kindness treat us as righteous.'

This is one of the earliest known Sequences, dating from about 850, and based on Jesus' parable of the Pharisee and the Publican (Luke 18.9–14). The poet's imagination brings the scene in the Temple to life by his skilful sketching-in of details, such as the tears on the Publican's face. He dares to call the penitent's example 'holy'; for him holiness consists, not in being good, but in responding to the undeserved goodness of God.

Stans a longe, OB p. 114. This translation first appeared in *Paths of the Heart* (London 1993), p. 56.

The melody of this Sequence is printed in Anselm Hughes, *Anglo-French Sequelae* (Farnborough 1966), p. 70. One of its titles, *Metensis minor*, suggests that it could possibly have originated at Metz, which was a musical 'centre of excellence' in the eighth and ninth centuries. The tune was also known as *Vitellia* and *Planctus publicani*. Twenty-three Sequences were set to this melody; *Stans a longe* was sung at Limoges (tenth century), Winchester (*c.* 1000), Chichester, London, and York on the Eleventh Sunday after Trinity, when its source-parable was the Gospel of the day. The fourteenth-century Benedictine Missal from Whitby Abbey sets it for the feast of the ex-publican St Matthew. Of the fifteen Sunday Sequences in the Winchester Troper, this is the only one to have survived into the late Middle Ages.

Bible Sunday

(an alternative to Proper 25 on the Sunday between 23 and 29 October inclusive)

A prayer for deeper understanding

O Lord, You have made us and have given us life.
When we came from the font of baptism, we bore the cross on
    our foreheads;
because of this we do not fear the temptations of evil,
but we revere You alone, O Lord, the Saviour of all.

Through Your only Son, we pray that You will open our hearts
to understand the words which speak of Your wisdom.

Grant us, in Your mercy, the grace of the Holy Spirit:
the Spirit of wisdom and understanding,
the Spirit of counsel and strength,
the Spirit of knowledge and holiness,
and fill us with the Spirit of reverence for You,
who have formed us from earth's clay,
and have redeemed us by Your own blood.

This prayer from the notebook of an eleventh-century Saxon nun is based on the description in Isaiah 11.2 of the Spirit which will rest upon the Messiah. In John 16.13 Jesus promises that the Spirit will lead his disciples into all truth. Like all good teachers, the Spirit does this gently and gradually, according to our ability to see truths and to grasp them. In our use of the Bible we need His grace to keep our minds open: as our experience of life deepens, so does our capacity to gain fresh insights into the mystery of God. Asking for His inspiration is no mere formality. Austin Farrer wrote that God 'takes the form of our action when he inspires us, when we let our will be the instrument of his. To realise a union with our Creator we need not scale heaven or strip the veil from ultimate mystery; for God descends into his creature and acts humanly in mankind'. (*A Science of God?*, London 1966, p. 127.)

Domine qui, a prayer in a manuscript from Winchester's 'Nunnaminster' (see p. 73–74), PC p. 87.
    This prayer is incomplete because of damage to the manuscript, which is the prayer's only known source.

Dedication Festival

(Last Sunday after Trinity or First Sunday in October, if the actual
date of Dedication is unknown)

Either: see 'Eighth Sunday in Ordinary Time, Year B', *The
spiritual marriage*, p. 50;

or: *Sharing the worship of heaven*

Let the Church, pure mother and spotless virgin,
sing in honour of this church.

This house is shown to be joined in fellowship with the
    heavenly hall
in the praise and worship of the King of heaven.
Its continually-burning lights
imitate the city where there is no darkness,
and it cherishes in its bosom
the bodies of those whose souls live in paradise.
Long may it give praise to God,
protected by His right hand!

Here grace, made fruitful by the Holy Spirit,
brings to birth a new offspring;
here dwellers in the angel-citadels come to visit their kindred,
and the body of Jesus is received.

All things that may harm the body flee away;
the sins of the guilty soul perish.
Here the voice of gladness rings out;
here peace and joy abound.
This house resounds always with the praise and glory of the
    Trinity.

NOTKER sees our worship of God and our celebration of the sacraments in earthly churches as a participation in the worshipping life of
the heavenly Church.

Psallat ecclesia, Notker's Sequence for the Dedication of a Church
(see pp. 24 and 25), NP p. 72 (melody on p. 93).
    Notker set this, his second attempt at Sequence-writing, to a West
Frankish melody, that is, one from the area which would later be

called 'France'. The tune is named *Laetatus sum* after the opening verse of Psalm 122 'I was glad when they said unto me: We will go into the house of the Lord'. In France this was the Alleluia-verse for the Second Sunday of Advent, and it was followed by this melody, sung to the Sequence *Regnantem sempiterna*. The verse is clearly suitable for a Dedication Festival, which is probably why Notker chose this melody for his Dedication Sequence. It is discussed by R. L. Crocker in *The Early Medieval Sequence* (Berkeley 1977) pp. 345–56, but Crocker's translation of *Psallat ecclesia* should be viewed with scepticism, as he seems to have mistaken several indicative verbs for subjunctive ones!

Psallat was the usual Dedication Sequence in Germany, and it appears in England as one of several alternatives for this feast in some Sarum manuscripts, as well as at Hereford and Chichester.

The feast originates from Pope Boniface IV's dedication of Agrippa's temple, the Pantheon, as the church of Sancta Maria ad Martyres in 608. It was the earliest of the post-Gregorian Roman feasts and came north of the Alps with the earliest layer of Roman liturgy introduced by the Carolingians. At first it was kept as the Dedication of S. Maria ad Martyres on 13 May, but its position in the Calendar soon became variable when it was used as the Dedication Feast of each individual church. In conservative southern Italy, however, it remained on 13 May until the thirteenth century. For details of its early repertoire of Tropes and Sequences, see Alejandro Planchart, 'An Aquitanian Sequentia in Italian Sources' in W. Arlt and G. Björkvall (eds.), *Recherches nouvelles sur les Tropes Liturgiques* (Stockholm 1993).

Fourth Sunday before Advent – Thirty-First Sunday in Ordinary Time

(Sunday between 30 October and 5 November inclusive)

Year A: see 'Proper 5, Year B', *Sharing the life of God*, p. 102.

Year B: see 'Proper 10, Year C', *Loving God and our neighbour*, p. 113.

Year C: see 'Proper 19, Year C', *The God who seeks the lost*, p. 125.

Or: All Saints' Sunday

(if the Feast was not celebrated on 1 November)

The joy of the saints

Let us offer to Christ the beauty of our praises,
for he adorns his saints with an eternal crown.

Full of splendour is the hall of heaven's glory:
there the great light of Godhead is servant to all,
bringing them their joyful rewards.

Holy peace and perfect love are there;
shining like gold, the people flourish as the spring-time.
No night is there, but all are bathed in the radiance of perpetual
day.
There is life without death or disease;
all are youthful, vigorous, and lovely.

Thousands of angels in sweet-sounding companies delight to
praise God,
eagerly crying out 'Holy, holy, holy' throughout the ages.
The streets sparkle with gleaming gold;
stupendous walls rise up, built of precious jewels.

There the saints whose festival we celebrate
shine resplendent, wreathed in glory.
May we be led there, helped by their prayers.

This tenth-century poet expresses the glory of the saints in imagery derived from Hebrews 12.22 and from the vision of the holy city in Revelation 21.18–26. He also adds a striking image of his own: that of God as the servant at the heavenly banquet, who fulfils the guests' needs and brings them gifts which make their joy complete.

Laude Christum, a Sequence for feasts of Virgins in the Oxford manuscript (Bodley 775) of the Winchester Troper (see p. 63), YM p. 309.

This is one the many Sequences written to the melody *Adducentur* (see p. 49), which at Winchester was also known as *Dulcedine paradisi*. It is printed in Dom Anselm Hughes' *Anglo-French Sequelae* (Farnborough 1966) on pp. 80–91.

Laude Christum, a typical product of the Winchester school, does not seem to have been sung elsewhere.

St John Chrysostom (d. 407) mentions the feast of All Saints as being celebrated on the Sunday after Pentecost, which it still is in the Eastern Church. This date is also found in the West in lectionaries from Würzburg and Murbach dating from the seventh and eighth centuries. There is evidence that it was observed in eighth century Britain on 1 November, possibly as a Christianization of the pagan Celtic festival of Samhain, when the flocks were brought down to the valley pastures for the winter, and sacred fires were lit to promote their fertility and to ward off the malevolent spirits of the dead. Alternatively, the 1 November date may have more to do with the dedication on that day of a chapel of All Saints in St Peter's Basilica by Pope Gregory III (d. 741). During the pontificate of Gregory IV (827–44) Charlemagne's son Louis the Pious ordered the feast to be kept on this date throughout the Carolingian Empire.

Third Sunday before Advent – Remembrance Sunday

(Sunday between 6 and 12 November inclusive.) If Remembrance Sunday should fall on the 2nd Sunday before Advent, see 'Fifth Sunday of Easter, Year C', *Christ who creates us anew*, p. 85.

A soldier's lament

'Fontenoy' the local people call their village and its spring.
Now the land recoils in horror at the dreadful slaughtering:
all its fields and woods and marshlands Frankish blood is
    watering.

Let the rain and dew of heaven wet those grassy fields no more;
fields where brave men, skilled in battle, fell, and bitter death-
    throes bore.
Parents, sisters, friends, and brothers grieve for them in anguish
    sore.

War should not be celebrated in heroic songs of praise;
rather let the whole earth sorrow, and its lamentations raise
for the men who fell in battle when the sword cut short their
    days.

In these fields of desolation stripped and bare the corpses lie;
vultures, crows, and wolves devour them: no fine tombs when
    these men die.
Let us seek their souls' well-being, praying to the Lord Most
    High.

We expect medieval war-poems to be celebrations of heroism in battle, but this one anticipates the sentiments of the First World War poets by almost 1100 years. It was written by Angilbert, a soldier in Lothair's army, which was defeated at the Battle of Fontenoy-en-Puisaye, near Auxerre, in 841. This was a time when Charlemagne's grandsons quarrelled bitterly over the division of the Holy Roman Empire. In verse 2 Angilbert alludes to David's lament over Saul and Jonathan in 2 Samuel 1.21. His own lament bewails the terrible suffering which is the result of war: the waste of young lives, and the anguish of grieving loved ones. He ends with an invitation to entrust the fallen to God's care.

Fontaneto fontem from *Aurora cum primo*, OB p. 111.

This is an alphabetical poem, each verse beginning with a letter of the alphabet from A to P. It is written in rhythmical trochaic tetrameters. We know nothing about its author apart from what he tells us in the poem: that he was called Angilbert, and that after fighting in this battle he stood alone in the front line.

On 25 June 841 Louis the German and Charles the Bald, younger sons of Louis the Pious (Charlemagne's son, who had died the previous year), inflicted a crushing defeat on Lothair, their elder brother.

Angilbert the soldier is not to be confused with the earlier Angilbert who was lay-abbot of St Riquier and organized the Rogation Processions mentioned on p. 90. Charlemagne, who loved to give classical nick-names to his friends at court, called him 'Homer' and he was also the 'boyfriend' of the Emperor's daughter Bertha (Charlemagne did not allow his daughters to marry!). Their son Nithard became Angilbert's successor as abbot.

Thirty-Second Sunday in Ordinary Time

(Sunday between 6 and 12 November)

Year A: see 'Eighth Sunday in Ordinary Time, Year B', *The spiritual marriage*, p. 50.

Year B: see 'Good Friday', *Our ransom*, p. 69.

Year C: see 'Proper 5, Year C', *Christ our Resurrection*, p. 103.

Second Sunday before Advent – Thirty-Third Sunday in Ordinary Time

(Sunday between 13 and 19 November inclusive. If today is Remembrance Sunday, see *A soldier's lament*, p. 137.)

Years A, B, and C: see 'Fifth Sunday of Easter, Year C', *Christ who creates us anew*, p. 85.

Christ the King

(Sunday between 20 and 26 November inclusive)

The royal splendour

O Lord, shining King of heaven's citadel,
save Your people in Your loving kindness.
The choirs of Cherubim unceasingly proclaim Your glory;
the noble Seraphim respond with hymns of praise.
The nine angelic orders worship You in their beauty;
the Church throughout the world unites to sing to You;
the sun, moon, and stars, the earth and sea all serve You,
O Christ the King, enthroned on high.

Gracious Son of the Virgin Mary, King of kings, blessed
   Redeemer,
You have ransomed us from the power of death with Your own
   blood.
O Sun of justice, when You come in Your shining splendour to
   judge the nations,
show Your tender mercy to us Your people.

The earthly enthronement of Christ, the King of all Creation, was upon the gibbet of the Cross. His royal power lies in the humility of his merciful love.

Rex splendens, a Trope to the *Kyrie eleison* in the Sarum, York, and Hereford Missals, YM p. 245.

A plainsong setting of the Mass uses the melody of this Trope for the *Kyrie*. In the Plainsong and Medieval Music Society's edition of *Missa Rex Splendens* (1908, p. 3) a delightful legend is recounted attributing the Trope's origin to St Dunstan (d. 988), Abbot of Glastonbury and Archbishop of Canterbury. The story goes that King Edgar had gone hunting one Sunday morning, and had asked his archbishop to delay saying Mass until he returned. The saint was waiting vested at the altar when he had a vision of heavenly worship with angels singing this *Kyrie*-Trope to the Trinity. When the king finally arrived, Dunstan told him that he had already heard Mass and would not celebrate another that day. He forbade the king to hunt any more on a Sunday, and he taught the chant he had heard sung in heaven to his clerks. Unfortunately, the story is almost certainly false! (See D. Hiley, *Western Plainchant*, Oxford 1993, p. 581.)

Kyrie Rex splendens may in fact be French. It appears as *Kyrie resplendens* in a mid-twelfth-century Troper from St Evroult in south-west Normandy. Margot Fassler points out (*Gothic Song*, Cambridge 1993, p. 94) that when this abbey was founded in 1050 much of its chant came from Chartres.

Part II

Saints' Days and Festivals

1 January – Solemnity of Mary

See '25 March – Annunciation', *The lion and the lamb*, p. 155.

1 January – Naming of Jesus

Name of sweetness

> True delight of heart and mind,
> deepest love in all creation,
> Jesus, joy of humankind,
> this world's glory and salvation.
>
> Jesus, name above all names,
> balsam-sweet and sense-entrancing;
> brighter than the sun it flames,
> Love, all other loves enhancing.
>
> Turn to us, who love your name
> and our hearts' devotion render;
> death, our foe, you overcame;
> now you share your Father's splendour.
>
> King of heaven, your reign brings peace:
> peace beyond our comprehending;
> deepest longings find release
> through your love, which knows no ending.

Dwelling on the name of a loved one is a process which can sometimes allow us to contemplate their nature. Their name, as we repeat it to ourselves, contains something of the unique essence of their personality. Human lovers know this when they are absent from each other, and many Christians find that repeating the name of Jesus slowly and attentively is a way of realizing the presence of Incarnate Love himself.

Tu mentis delectatio from *Dulcis Jesu memoria*, OB p. 352.
    As well as dwelling on the sweetness of the beloved name, this Cistercian poet alludes to its meaning, as revealed by the angel to St Joseph in Matthew 1.21 'You shall call his name Jesus, for he will save his people from their sins'.
    A subtle change in the flavour of Christian devotion took place in Europe during the twelfth century. Jesus in his tender and vulnerable

humanity became the focus of many hymns and prayers from this time onwards; Christians expressed their love for God with a new warmth and romanticism which owed much to the writings of St Bernard of Clairvaux (1090–1153) and the Cistercian Order. Ascetic living and romantic religious writing often seemed to go together at this period!

Later in the Middle Ages aspects of Christ's humanity were celebrated in public worship: there was a Mass of the Sacred Face of Christ, and a Mass of the Five Wounds. In England one of the most popular of these devotions was that to the Holy Name of Jesus. Late in the fourteenth century this became a liturgical feast, kept on 7 August. Many churches had Jesus Altars and Jesus Guilds, whose purpose was to give honour to the Holy Name. In Durham Cathedral the Jesus Altar was particularly prominent, being immediately in front of the great Rood Screen. It had its own vestments, choir-loft, and organ; the Mass of the Holy Name (called the 'Jesus Mass') was sung there every Friday. (See R.W. Pfaff, *New Liturgical Feasts in Later Medieval England*, Oxford 1970, pp. 62–83.)

A Sequence frequently sung at this Mass was *Dulcis Jesu memoria*, sometimes called the 'Rosy Sequence'. The first part of it is familiar as the hymn 'Jesu, the very thought of thee'; some verses from the latter part of it are translated here. The poem is very much in the style of St Bernard and used to be attributed to him. It is now thought to have been written by an English Cistercian at the end of the twelfth century.

6 January – Epiphany

Royal gifts

Let us praise the Lord for his glorious Epiphany,
when the Wise Men worshipped the Son of God.
The prophets foretold that he should come
to save all the nations of the world.

He humbled his royal power and stooped down low,
taking upon himself the form of a servant;
though he was God before time began,
he was made man, and born of Mary.

He is the shining star which Balaam prophesied should rise out
    of Jacob,
and crush the forces of the enemy by his great might.

With the star to guide them, flashing its fire,
the Wise Men bring to him their splendid gifts:
gold, and incense, and myrrh.

Incense proclaims him as God,
gold as a great king,
and myrrh as a mortal man, doomed to die.

Let us in spirit offer to Christ, the King of kings, our own
    precious gifts,
and ask him to keep the world and all its people in his eternal
    protection.

Balaam's prophecy about the star is in Numbers 24.17: 'A star shall come forth out of Jacob, and a sceptre shall rise out of Israel: it shall crush the forehead of Moab ...'

The poet sees the Epiphany star both as an image of God's guidance and also, by linking it with the star in Balaam's prophecy, as a sign that Jesus is the promised Messiah. His Messiahship, though, is not a nationalistic one, crushing human enemies by physical strength. The Epiphany celebrates the revelation of Jesus as the Saviour of the whole human race, not just of one section of it, and he liberates us from our common human enemies of sin and death. He does this by following the path of humility and obedience. The poet alludes to St Paul's great hymn to Christ's humility in Philippians 2.5ff.: 'Though he was in the form of God, (Jesus) did not count equality with God a thing to be grasped, but emptied himself, taking the form of a servant.'

In the last part of the poem the writer takes up another Epiphany theme, the Wise Men's symbolic gifts to the Christ-child. He invites his fellow-Christians to offer their own precious gifts to Christ, and hints that the most precious thing we can offer is the gift of ourselves. Offering ourselves to God involves identifying ourselves with God's care and concern for all His creation, and so the poem ends with an invitation to pray for the well-being of the world and all its people.

Epiphaniam Domino, SM p. 465.

This poem dates from the tenth century. It was the Sequence sung in nearly all the major churches of England and France on the Feast of the Epiphany. In York Minster, and in those churches in northern England which followed the Use of York, it was divided into three sections, each of which was assigned to the first three days of the Epiphany Octave. Parts of the opening lines of these second and third sections (*Balaam de quo vaticinans* and *Stella micante praevia*) were incorporated into a fifteenth-century carol 'Make we joy', published in the *Oxford Book of Carols*. This is an indication of how popular the piece still was in England, even five hundred years after it was written.

25 January – Conversion of St Paul

Turning to the light

We celebrate today the conversion of St Paul,
whom the Lord made rich with so many gifts of grace
that the whole Church calls him the Teacher of the Nations.

The wolf becomes a lamb:
the persecutor becomes an evangelist.

The heavenly light which shines around him takes away his sight
but gives him spiritual insight.

Heaven strikes him in his pride:
lays him low, but lifts him up;
casts him down, but corrects him;
in correcting him, heals him;
encourages him to learn by faith;
sets him up to defend that Church
which before he had attacked.

Now Paul goes through all the world,
preaching the hidden wisdom he has learned.

This eleventh-century poet is alive to the contrasts in the story of
Paul's conversion, in which the Church's greatest persecutor becomes
the Apostle to the Gentiles. Struck blind by the light of Truth, he
learns that his aggressive assertion of the rightness of his views was a
cloak to hide his spiritual blindness. John Betjeman suggests that Paul
asked himself 'And do you think that you are strong/Enough to own
that you were wrong?' Betjeman adds: 'What is Conversion? Turning
round/To gaze upon a love profound.' Even sudden conversions are
part of a process of seeing further into the depths of God's love.

Selected verses from *Sancti Pauli conversio*, YM p. 14.
    Apart from the first three words, this is the same Sequence as
Sollemnitas sancti Pauli. It is first found in an eleventh-century manuscript from Cambrai but seems to have been used mainly in England,
where it occurs in thirteen Uses, set both for this feast and for the
Commemoration of St Paul on 30 June. The York Missal adapted the
opening words to make it more especially appropriate for today's
festival. It survived into the sixteenth-century printed missals of

Sarum, York and Hereford, as well as those of some northern French dioceses. At York it appears as an alternative to *Dixit Dominus Ex Basan* which is the usual German Sequence for this feast, probably written by Gottschalk of Aachen (see pp. 107–108). The melody for *Sancti Pauli* was called *Lyra* or *Ecce pulchra*; it is given by Dom Anselm Hughes in *Anglo-French Sequelae* (Farnborough 1966), p. 53.

Today's feast originated in Gaul, where it is mentioned in the eighth century.

The quotations from John Betjeman come from his poem 'The Conversion of St Paul' in *Uncollected Poems* (London 1982), pp. 67–70.

2 February – Presentation of Christ

Mary's offering

Virgin Mother,
you brought with you to the temple for purification
him who gave you in abundance integrity's glory:
God, born as a human child.

Rejoice, holy Mary!
He who searches our hearts and our inmost being
found you alone a worthy dwelling for himself.
O Mary, be joyful,
because your little one, who then smiled up at you,
has made us all secure and happy in his love.

As we keep this feast
of Christ, made a small child for our sake,
and of his holy mother Mary,
though we, slow-hearted,
cannot match God's great humility,
let us take his mother as our guide.

Praise to the Father of glory
who, in revealing His Son to Israel and the nations,
unites us with the company of His People.
Praise also to His only Son
who, in reconciling us to the Father by his own blood,
has united us with the citizens on high.
Praise also be to the Holy Spirit throughout all ages.

The secure and happy love which we see in the faces of Mother and
Child in NOTKER'S poem is God's gift to us all, for that Child
embodies the love of God.

Ad templum from *Concentu parili*, Notker's Sequence for Candlemas
in his *Liber hymnorum* (see pp. 24–25), NP p. 22.
　　The blessing of candles at today's feast seems to have reminded
Notker of that other great service of light, the Easter Vigil: the
opening words of this Sequence are a quotation from a fourth-
century poem by Prudentius, *Inventor rutili*, which was often
sung in the Middle Ages on Holy Saturday while the procession
returned to the chancel after the blessing of the New Fire and

the lighting of the Paschal Candle.

Notker did not use a French (West Frankish) melody for *Concentu parili*, as he had done for *Psallat ecclesia*. The tune, called *Symphonia*, is printed and discussed in R. L. Crocker, *The Early Medieval Sequence* (Berkeley 1977), pp. 228ff.

Concentu parili was the usual Sequence for this feast in Germany, and it appears in some Sarum manuscripts as an alternative to *Hac clara die*. It also occurs in England at Winchester, Sherborne, and in the 'Caligula Troper' (BL Calig. A xiv), which some scholars assign to Canterbury and some to Hereford.

The writings of the fourth-century pilgrim Egeria show that there was a feast at that time in Jerusalem on this fortieth day after Christmas. In the East it is known as *Hypapante*, or 'Meeting', and refers to the meeting of Simeon with his Lord. Pope Sergius I, whose ancestry was Syrian, introduced this Eastern feast into the Roman liturgy in the late seventh century. The origins of today's procession may lie in the pagan lustrations of the walls of Rome, called *Amburbale*.

19 March – St Joseph

Humble contentment

Christ, the Church's heavenly bridegroom,
came to us in secret guise;
taking flesh in Mary's body,
hidden from all human eyes.
Mystery of Incarnation,
which God's wisdom did devise.

Joseph's troubled mind was quietened
as he slept at midnight's hour:
in his dreams an angel told him
that the Holy Spirit's power
all mysteriously was working,
blessings on the world to shower.

Child and Mother he accepted,
loved them with devotion true;
living humbly in contentment
while the Child in wisdom grew;
and at last, his life's work over,
gained the crown that was his due.

This poet emphasizes the hiddenness of God's work in the Incarnation of His Son: the months lying hidden in Mary's womb, and the years living in humble obscurity in Nazareth. He celebrates Joseph's trust in God, despite his natural perplexity at Mary's pregnancy. Joseph is an example of the great things God can do when people consent to His will for them: by faithfulness to his undramatic domestic vocation, he played a vital part in God's saving purposes.

Selected verses from *Christus ecclesiae*, LS p. 262.

This Sequence is found in the 'Codex Brander' (St Gall Ms. 546), a sumptuously produced anthology compiled at the famous Swiss abbey in 1507.

Joseph was a curiously neglected saint during most of the Middle Ages. There are faint traces of a liturgical commemoration of him in the ninth century: his name appears under 19 March in two copies of a Martyrology from the island monastery of Reichenau on Lake Constance. Devotion to him was fostered in the thirteenth century among Franciscans and Carmelites, but it was not until the pontificate of Sixtus IV (1471–84) that his feast was admitted into the Calendar. *Christus ecclesiae* may well date from that time.

25 March – Annunciation

The lion and the lamb

Through the Angel's greeting
at that happy meeting
came down sweet salvation.

Sun from star proceeding,
you, God's promise heeding,
brought the New Creation.

Wonder beyond telling,
you became the dwelling
of the Saviour holy,
Virgin poor and lowly,
blest above all other.

Lamb, so small and tender,
lion in his splendour,
the faithful shepherd true,
God's manna, flower, and dew
chose you as his mother.

From a certain angle, the rock-formation on the top of Helm Crag, near Grasmere in the Lake District, looks like a lion standing next to a lamb. As one moves along the road from Ambleside to Keswick the perspective changes, and the same group of rocks begins to resemble a witch hunched over her cauldron, and then a cannon pointing skywards. In a similar way, this poet has brought together a number of contrasting images in order to express something of the many-sided mystery of the Incarnation, when the splendour of God was revealed on earth as a tiny helpless baby, and the Divine Wisdom chose a village girl to be his mother.

Per hoc autem from *Ave Maria gratia plena*, YM p. 83.
  This Marian Sequence was widespread in Germany, and is found in French sources from Nevers and Paris. In the cathedral of Notre Dame it was set for today's festival, while at the abbey of St Denis it was sung at the Saturday Mass of Our Lady in the season after Pentecost. In England it occurs in eleven Uses, of which the earliest witness is BL Roy. 2 B iv from St Albans, *c.* 1140. (Anselm Hughes is mistaken, in *Anglo-French Sequelae* p. 132, in including the eleventh-

century Leofric Collectar from Exeter among its sources.) English choirs tended to sing it on one of the days in the Octave of the Assumption.

Being nine months before Christmas Day, the observance of this feast was a logical consequence of the adoption of 25 December as the feast of the Nativity. It entered the Calendar at some time between the fifth and seventh centuries, making its first appearance in the Western Church in the Gelasian Sacramentary.

31 May – Visitation

Guided by grace

Come to us and visit us,
Mary, Holy Spirit's bride;
may God's love, which shone in you,
brighten us and be our guide.

To the house of Zachary
you were led by grace divine;
may that grace give strength to us,
and within our spirits shine.

Star whose radiance calms the sea,
bring us peace and sweet accord;
let our hearts leap up with joy,
as John leapt to greet his Lord.

May God's Spirit guide our lives,
as in you His will was done;
that our thoughts and words and deeds
may give glory to your Son.

In *Le Milieu Divin* Teilhard de Chardin said 'Cleanse your intention, and the least of your actions will be filled with God'. If we try to want what God wants, He will be able to work creatively through our being simply and naturally ourselves. The Visitation story shows God's grace at work through Mary's natural inclination as a young mother-to-be to seek the support and companionship of her older cousin. In its own way, her following of this gracious prompting was as much of a 'Yes' to God as her obedient response at the Annunciation, and, as God's grace typically does, it led to unlooked-for blessings for both women.

Selected verses from the Sequence *Veni praecelsa Domina*, YM p. 232.

The Visitation is unusual among late medieval feasts in that it began not from a Votive Mass, as did the Holy Name, but from a papal decree. It was instituted by Boniface IX in 1389 but in many places, including England, it was not generally observed until after a further papal edict by Sixtus IV in 1475. (It was this Sixtus, a Franciscan, who brought the feast of St Joseph into the Calendar – see p. 154.)

There was some variation as to the date on which the Visitation was kept: in most places, including Sarum, it was 2 July, but at York it was observed on 2 April. The usual Sarum Sequence was *Celebremus in hac die; Veni praecelsa* is found at Hereford and in a late fifteenth-century manuscript of the York Missal.

There is a detailed account of the feast's history in R.W. Pfaff, *New Liturgical Feasts in Later Medieval England* (Oxford 1970), pp. 40–61.

24 June – Birth of St John the Baptist

The Forerunner

Zachary's Elizabeth today brought forth a child who was
    destined for greatness;
even before he was born he sensed the presence of God
hidden in Mary's womb, like the kernel enclosed in the
    nutshell.

Later, his goodness shone forth through his simple life in the
    desert:
rough camel-hair for his clothes, his food wild honey and
    locusts.

Then, as the gospels declare, he proclaimed that Light which is
    Jesus;
he himself was not that Light, but merely a lantern
showing the way to the peace and joy of the kingdom of
    heaven.

This is the man who baptized the Christ, the Living Fountain
    of waters;
there in Jordan's stream the whole of Creation is cleansed.

So, as we keep this feast of your Forerunner and Baptist,
help us, O Christ, when the path of our life goes through dry
    desert places;
grant us to bring in our sheaves with joy to our well-watered
    homeland,
that fair land which we seek, where your peace and love are
    supreme.

This poet blends the description of the Baptist's ministry in the
prologue to St John's Gospel (1.8) with a verse from the psalms: 'I
have prepared a lantern for my Anointed' (Psalm 132.17). In the final
stanza, John's life in the desert becomes a symbol of the dry and desolate patches in our own lives. The writer prays that Christ will help us
to come through these periods in the wilderness, so that, like the
reapers in Psalm 126.6, we may finally bring in the harvest of our lives
with joy to our heavenly homeland.

Selected verses from *Helisabeth Zachariae*, LS p. 258.

Sequences never achieved the same level of popularity in Italy as they did in northern Europe, but this may be an Italian work – it is found in a Venice manuscript of the fourteenth century.

Some other verses of the same Sequence are translated above, set for the Third Sunday of Advent, p. 14.

The date of this festival was fixed at some time late in the fourth century by counting back six months from Christmas Day. (By Roman reckoning, 24 June is 8 days before the Kalends of July, and 25 December is 8 days before the Kalends of January.) St Augustine saw it as a Christianization of the pagan festival of the summer solstice. In the Gallican Church St John the Baptist was commemorated on 29 August, the date which is now kept as the feast of his Beheading. (This feast first appears in the Roman Calendar in the seventh century.)

29 June – SS Peter and Paul

Two paths to apostleship

O Eternal God, we give You thanks especially today
for Your blessed apostles and martyrs Peter and Paul.
In your graciousness You chose them and consecrated them to
　　Yourself.

You turned blessed Peter away from his earthly skills at
　　fishing,
and called him to the practice of heavenly wisdom,
so that he might set the human race free from the depths of
　　this world
by means of the net of Your teachings.

You changed the nature of his fellow-apostle Paul as well as
　　his name:
the Church once feared him as a persecutor;
now she rejoices to have him as a teacher of heavenly precepts.

Paul was made blind, so that he might see;
Peter denied, so that he might have faith.
To one You entrusted the keys of the kingdom of heaven;
to the other You granted heavenly wisdom for the teaching of
　　the nations.
Paul led people to the gates;
Peter opened them wide.
Both of them therefore now enjoy the eternal rewards of their
　　virtue.

God's ever-creative Spirit bestows a wonderful variety of gifts on His
people (1 Corinthians 12.4ff; Ephesians 4.11ff). Peter and Paul shared
a common vocation as apostles, but their temperaments could hardly
have been more different. Without such diversity, and its accompany-
ing tensions, the Church would be much poorer. For both of them,
however, their paths to apostleship led through humiliating weakness
and failure. Though devastating at the time, Paul's blindness and
Peter's denial broke the shell of their pride, opened them up to God's
grace, and enabled them to grow healthily into their true unique selves.

Praecipue hodie, the *Immolatio* or Proper Preface for this feast in the *Missale Gothicum* (see p. 26), MG p. 107.

See p. 38 for the way in which this prayer treats the close relationship between nature and grace.

29 June is given as the date of this feast in the oldest surviving Roman Calendar, dating from 354. It was probably the date on which the apostles' bodies were transferred to temporary tombs in the catacombs of St Sebastian in the Appian Way during the Valerian persecution in 258. The date was kept as a feast-day shared by both saints when their bodies were returned to their original resting-places.

3 July – St Thomas

see 'Second Sunday of Easter', *The upper room*, p. 80.

22 July – St Mary Magdalen

Herald of Easter joy

Early on the week's first morning the Son of God arose,
our hope and our glory.
He overcame the king of evil and came back from the dead
with a mighty victory.
Through his Resurrection all creatures find their consolation
and the fullness of joy.

Magdalen then became the Risen Christ's first herald;
she brought to his grief-stricken brothers
joys which their hearts could not hold.
How blest were her eyes when first they gazed on the King of
  the ages,
once laid dead in the tomb, now full of glorious life!

Christ in his grace had washed away all her sins
as she bathed his feet with her tears.
While she wept and prayed in her mind,
her deeds proclaimed that she loved her Lord above all things.

May the Fountain of supreme goodness, who washed Mary
  from her sins,
cleanse us his servants too, and grant us pardon.

Tradition identifies Mary Magdalen with the despised figure at the banquet in Luke 7.36ff, whose outpouring of penitent love was accepted and welcomed by Jesus. Embraced by God's mercy, she is entrusted with the mystery of Resurrection: the 'Little Apostle' (as Eastern Christians call her) is sent to spread the Good News which fills her heart.

Selected verses from *Mane prima*, SM p. 469.
    This Parisian Sequence dates from the second half of the eleventh century. It appears in England about the year 1140 in a St Albans manuscript (BL Roy. 2Biv) and in the Sarum Use it was sung both on today's feast and sometimes also on the Saturday in Easter week. The usual Sequence in Germany was Gottschalk of Aachen's *Laus tibi Christe*, part of which is translated above on p. 107. The York Use set *Mane prima* for Low Sunday and offered it on Mary Magdalen's Day as an alternative to *Laus tibi*. (York was much more partial to German Sequences than was the Use of Sarum.)

29 July – Mary, Martha, and Lazarus

(see 'Proper 11, Year C', *Mutual love and peace*, p. 114.

6 August – Transfiguration

(see 'Sunday next before Lent', *A glimpse of glory*, p. 52.

15 August – The Blessed Virgin Mary (Assumption)

A woman clothed with the sun

Mother and daughter of Eternal Might,
lantern that guides us, full of God's own light,
rose without blemish, ravishing our sight,
flower of Creation;

Heaven's high King, who reigns as God alone,
your Son, our Brother, shares with you his throne;
earth's contests won, he claims you as his own,
our blood-relation.

Mary's unique vocation to be the mother of the Messiah began at the Annunciation when she opened herself to receive the light of the Holy Spirit. That vocation culminated in her sharing, in common with all God's people, in the heavenly glory of her Son. Because of her special closeness to Jesus as his mother, Christians have thought of her as being especially close to the glorified Christ in heaven, and as being clothed in the rays of the Sun of Justice (cf. Revelation 12.1). This poet, possibly PETER ABÉLARD (1079–1142), sees Mary as our blood-relation: because as Christians we are the Body of Christ, Jesus' mother is our mother too. Each of us has a vocation to be a Christ-bearer in our own unique way, and, like her, we are heirs of eternal glory. Mary is a sign of the hope that all Creation will ultimately share the glory of Christ.

The opening verses of the Sequence *Aeterni numinis*, SM p. 495.
    The attribution of this piece to Abélard is a guess on my part, based on its metre, style, and vocabulary. The metre, rhythmical dactylic tetrameter, is an unusual one and is found in several of Abélard's known works including the famous *O quanta qualia* ('O what their joy and their glory must be') and his Good Friday hymn *Solus ad victimam* (translated in my *Paths of the Heart*, p. 36). He wrote a prefatory letter to Héloïse (printed in J.-P. Migne, *Patrologia Latina*, Vol. 178, col. 379) accompanying some sermons he had written for her nuns at the convent of the Paraclete near Nogent-sur-Seine, in which he mentions a 'book of hymns or Sequences' which she had requested. Most of the hymns survive (*ibid.*, cols. 1771–1816), but the manuscript unfortunately breaks off in the middle of the Office Hymn for St Mary Magdalen's Day, and so the part containing the Sequences no longer exists. The phrase 'hymns or Sequences' cannot

mean 'hymns which could also be used as Sequences' because the hymns are each assigned to a particular Office. The sense is rather 'a book which is a Hymnary when its first part is used for the Office, or a Sequentiary when its second part is used at Mass'.

Four of Abélard's *Planctûs* were used liturgically at Nevers, and the Sequence *Mittit ad Virginem* (widespread in France and England, and in a style and metre similar to *Aeterni numinis*) is ascribed to Abélard by the sixteenth-century Parisian writer Clichtoveus.

Aeterni numinis occurs in two of the thirteenth-century Sarum manuscripts in SM, in BL Cotton Caligula A xiv (Canterbury or Hereford), and in the Dublin Troper of *c*. 1360.

Today's feast was anciently called the *Dormitio* (Falling-asleep) of the Virgin Mary, and has an Eastern origin. It spread throughout the Western Church during the seventh and eighth centuries.

29 August – Beheading of St John the Baptist

see 'Second Sunday of Advent', *The herald's voice*, p. 12.

14 September – Holy Cross Day

The Tree of Life

Hail, holy Cross, most worthy tree!

Your wood's strong heart
bore the weight of the world's precious ransom;
our foe, once victor through a tree,
now by a tree is vanquished.

Though death sprang from you
when earth's first dwellers were banished from Paradise,
now, through the life-giving death of Christ,
you are the source of life for all.

You, holy Cross, are for ever the sign
that makes our fierce enemies tremble;
death fears you, hell you strike with terror,
by you Christ seals his people as his own.

To him be praise for ever.

The contrast between the tree which occasioned humanity's fall
(Genesis 3) and the tree of the Cross is found as early as the second
century. St Irenaeus said that Christ 'healed the disobedience enacted
on the tree by obedience on a tree'. The symbolism of the Cross as the
Tree of Life has a biological basis too: as a tree absorbs carbon
dioxide and gives off oxygen, so Jesus on the Cross absorbs the poison
of our sin by his compassionate forgiveness, and breathes new life into
us by the gift of his love.

The Sequence *Salve crux sancta*, YM p. 34.
The structure of this eleventh-century Sequence is typically
German, being: a, bb, cc, dd, e. The first and last strophes are single
versicles because their melody was not repeated, as it was in strophes
2 to 4. Anglo-French Sequences tended to consist entirely of syllabically parallel double-versicles, each involving a repetition of its
melodic phrase. *Salve crux* was widespread in Germany and Italy, and
is found in some French and at least fifteen English manuscripts. At
York it was sung on the feast of the Finding of the Cross (3 May),
while Hugh of Orléans' famous *Laudes crucis attollamus* was set for
today. (Part of this is translated in *Paths of the Heart*, p. 30.) At

Sarum both Sequences were given as options on both feasts.

The melody of *Salve crux*, called *Dulce lignum*, is unusual in that it simply re-uses the melody of the Gregorian Alleluia-verse from which it takes its name. The words of the Alleluia-verse ('Sweetest wood and sweetest iron ...') are a quotation from Venantius Fortunatus' hymn *Pange lingua* ('Sing, my tongue, the glorious battle'). The melody is given by Anselm Hughes in *Anglo-French Sequelae*, p. 37.

The quotation above from St Irenaeus comes from his *Adversus Haereses* 5. 16. 3. Irenaeus' idea of the tree as a link between Fall and Redemption is developed in the Preface from the Mass of the Holy Cross, which was clearly drawn upon by the author of *Salve crux*: '[God] ordained that humankind should be saved by the tree of the Cross; that whence death arose, thence life might also arise; and that he who by a tree overcame, might also by a tree be overcome.' The medieval love of a colourful story transformed this link into narrative. In his immensely popular *Golden Legend* the thirteenth-century Dominican Jacobus de Voragine recounts the tale that Adam's son Seth was given a shoot from the Tree of Life by an angel. He planted it in Adam's grave, and the Cross of Christ was eventually fashioned from the wood of the tree which grew there (ed. W. G. Ryan, Princeton 1993, Vol. I, p. 277).

21 September – St Matthew

see 'Proper 5, Year A', *The call of Matthew*, p. 100.

29 September – Michaelmas

Our unseen protectors

May God give us His blessing;
He is the source of the light in which the angels live;
He has created them to be His fellow-citizens
and companions around His heavenly throne.

May their ministry defend our lives on earth,
so that, freed from our enemies
both visible and invisible,
we may be worthy to come to our eternal rewards.

Among them we venerate especially the Archangel Michael;
may his help support us
as we devoutly celebrate his memory today here on earth,
so that we may enjoy his fellowship in the starry heavens.

May God, whose kingdom and power
last through all the ages of eternity,
grant us this blessing.

Human eyes can see most of the colours of the spectrum, but ultra-violet and infra-red elude our unaided sight. Similarly, the infinitely varied spectrum of God's creatures may well include beings who cannot be perceived by our normal senses. Angels, by tradition, adore God and protect humankind. They are also God's messengers, who, in the famous lines of Francis Thompson, reveal His many-splendoured presence all around us in the world:

'The angels keep their ancient places;
Turn but a stone, and start a wing!'
'Tis ye, 'tis your estrangèd faces,
That miss the many-splendour'd thing.'

Benedicat, the blessing for Michaelmas in the Benedictional of Archbishop Robert (see p. 20), BR p. 42.

The quotation from Francis Thompson comes from his much-anthologized poem 'In no Strange Land', sub-titled 'The Kingdom of God is within you.' It appears, for example, in A. Quiller-Couch (ed.), *The Oxford Book of English Verse*, New Edition (Oxford 1939), p. 1049.

Today's feast was originally the dedication festival of the church of

San Michele in the Via Salaria in Rome. It is found in the Verona Sacramentary (the so-called 'Leonine'), which dates from the early seventh century, but contains older material.

1 November – All Saints' Day

see 'All Saints' Sunday', *The joy of the saints*, p. 136.

2 November – All Souls' Day

Cherishing those who have died

O Eternal God,
the whole Church acknowledges You
as one Deity in three Persons;
You are always ready to give healing and immortal life
to those who have died.
Look favourably on the prayers which Your faithful people
    make to You on behalf of their departed loved ones.

While they were on earth
You redeemed them with the blood of Your only Son,
and You cherished and protected them by Your Holy Spirit.

Free them from all their sins;
let the grace of the Spirit warm them with its rays;
crown them among the saints in the starry heights
where You live the perfect life of the Trinity
in glory for ever.

This prayer contains the image of God's life-giving Spirit as a fire: not
a consuming one, but a cheerful one, blazing in a hearth on a winter's
day. We can picture our departed loved ones warming themselves at
it, having come in from the cold, and being given new life and fresh
hope as they bathe in the radiance of God's merciful love. Then the
domestic scene changes to one of celestial splendour: as members of
God's royal and priestly people, their final destiny is to be crowned
among the saints in the glory of heaven.

Deus quem, a prayer for All Souls' Day in the Benedictional of
Archbishop Robert (see p. 20), BR p. 56.

All Souls's Day began as a local observance in the abbey of Cluny.
In 998 Abbot Odilo ordered it to be kept in all Cluny's dependent
monasteries, and, because of the great influence of the Cluniac Order,
it soon spread throughout the Western Church.

26 December – St Stephen

The martyr's crown

God gave a crown to blessed Stephen the first martyr
because he bravely proclaimed his faith
and was victorious in the conflict of his martyrdom.
May God also encircle our hearts
with the crown of justice in this present world,
and in the world to come
lead us to the crown of eternal glory.

By His gracious gift
may we always be aglow with love for God and our neighbour:
that love which Stephen showed with eager joy,
even in the midst of the assaults
of those who were stoning him.

May Stephen's prayers strengthen us
and his example sustain us,
and may Christ, whom he saw standing at the right hand of God,
grant us his blessing.

There are striking similarities between St Luke's account of the
martyrdom of Stephen in Acts and the Passion Story in his Gospel.
Stephen says 'Lord, lay not this sin to their charge' (Acts 7.60), and
Jesus says 'Father, forgive them' (Luke 23.34); Stephen's 'Lord Jesus,
receive my spirit' (7.59) echoes Christ's words 'Father, into thy hands
I commend my spirit' (23.46). Luke makes these connections between
the two narratives to show that Jesus lives on and acts typically in the
members of his Body, the Church. For Jesus the reward of faithfulness
was a crown of thorns, and the same is true metaphorically for his
followers in every age. But an eternal crown awaits them, and in the
midst of their suffering his presence and his strength are with them.

Deus qui beatum Stephanum, the blessing for St Stephen's Day in the
Benedictional of Archbishop Robert (see p. 20), BR p. 33.

The imagery of crowning pervades this prayer because Stephen's
name (*Stephanos* in Greek) means 'crown'.

Durandus, the Bishop of Mende and a popular commentator on the
liturgy in the thirteenth century, called St Stephen, St John, and the
Holy Innocents the *comites Christi*, the 'companions of Christ',
because their feasts fall on the three days following Christmas Day. St

Stephen's feast is found in the seventh-century Roman sacramentaries (Gregorian, Gelasian, and Verona/'Leonine'), and the writings of St Gregory of Nyssa provide evidence of its observance in the East in the fourth century.

For more details of the correspondences between St Luke's Gospel and the Acts of the Apostles see M.D. Goulder, *Type and History in Acts* (London 1964), Chapter 3.

27 December – St John

The beloved disciple

We give You thanks, Almighty God,
as we celebrate the heavenly birthday of blessed John,
Your apostle and evangelist.

He received his calling from our Lord Jesus Christ, Your Son:
he no longer caught fish,
but with his pen and its saving doctrines
he rescued souls who had been sunk
in the swirling waters of the world.

At the holy supper, that mystic banquet,
he leaned on the breast of his saviour,
and on the Cross the Lord made him
the adopted son of his Virgin Mother.

He was the first to show by his teaching
that the Word was with God in the beginning,
and that the Word was truly divine.

The author of this seventh-century prayer compares and contrasts St John's activity before and after his calling by Jesus. Instead of the net with which he 'rescued' fish from the sea, he wields his pen, by which he saves souls from the treacherous depths of the world. The writer uses 'world' in the sense often employed by John in his Gospel, in which it means not 'the world as created by God' but 'human life as organized apart from God'. He follows the tradition of identifying St John with the beloved disciple who learned on Jesus' breast at supper (13.23) and was entrusted to Mary in a bond of mutual care (19.26f). He ends by celebrating again the teachings which flowed from the saint's pen in the sublime opening verses of the Gospel's prologue.

Beati Johannis, part of the *Immolatio* (Preface) for the feast of St John on 6 May in the *Missale Gothicum* (see p. 26), MG p. 94.

As happened in the case of John the Baptist (see p. 160), the old Gallican date of John the Apostle's feast, 6 May, became a lesser feast in his honour in the Roman Rite: St John *ante Portam Latinam* commemorated a story told in the second-century apocryphal *Acts of John* in which the saint is thrown into a cauldron of boiling oil at the orders of the Emperor Domitian, but emerges unscathed. The incident is supposed to have taken place 'before the Latin Gate', that is, the gate leading southwards from Rome to Latium. The Gallican Church followed the Eastern practice of commemorating the brothers James and John together on 27 December.

The delightful German custom of blessing and distributing *Johanneswein* today is thought to derive from the practice, adapted from paganism, of sharing a 'loving-cup' in honour of certain saints.

Another part of this *Immolatio* is translated above on p. 38.

28 December – Holy Innocents

The martyr-flowers

In this yearly festival we remember the sufferings
and celebrate the memory of those children
who were torn away from their nursing mothers' breasts
by Herod's henchmen.

They are rightly called 'martyr-flowers',
for they burst forth, the Church's first jewels,
and sprang up like a bright fountain in the town of Bethlehem;
but they appeared in the midst of a winter of treachery,
and were shrivelled by the frost of persecution.

Though they were children too young to speak,
they sounded the Lord's praises with joy.
Their blood proclaimed in death what their tongues could not
     express in life.
No word was on their tongues, yet they were granted the honour
     of martyrdom.

The infant Christ sent them on before him,
his forerunners to heaven.

In his treatment of the slaughter of the Innocents (Matthew 2.16) the
author of this prayer from seventh-century Gaul quotes a phrase from
the hymn 'All hail, ye little martyr-flowers' by the fourth-century poet
Prudentius. This image of the young martyrs as flowers develops
vividly in the writer's imagination: a flower springing up and opening
its petals reminds him of a fountain whose waters gush upwards,
sparkling like jewels, and then fall to the ground. The cruelty which
killed those tender plants is compared to the harshness of a winter
frost. The writer alludes to a verse from the Psalms to express their
wordless worship of God: 'Out of the mouth of babes and sucklings
thou hast perfected praise' (Psalm 8.2, Vulgate).

Annua festivitate, the *Immolatio* (Preface) for the Holy Innocents in
the *Missale Gothicum* (see p. 26), MG p. 15.
     In the East the Apostles Peter and Paul are celebrated today, but in
the West the Holy Innocents have been commemorated on 28
December since the fifth century.
     The text of Prudentius' *Salvete, flores martyrum* (part of his
Cathemerinon) is in OB p. 24.

Feasts of Apostles

see 'Proper 6, Year A', *The calling of the Twelve*, p. 105.

Feasts of Evangelists

Life-giving waters

> Four streams through Eden's garden flow,
> causing living things to grow;
> trees and plants their blossoms show,
> joyful in life's fertile force.
>
> These streams flow from Christ, the spring;
> down from heaven his grace they bring,
> to his people offering
> health and sweetness from life's source.
>
> Those who to these waters throng
> find their thirst grows still more strong;
> tasting love, for love they long,
> and for its fulfilment sigh.
>
> May we to their teaching cleave,
> and sin's tainted waters leave,
> and be drawn, as we believe,
> closer to our home on high.

This twelfth-century poet uses the image of the river flowing out of
Eden (Genesis 2.10) as a symbol of the life-giving love of God. Those
who drink from this stream find satisfaction and yet, paradoxically,
also long for love's deeper fulfilment. This is the living water which
Jesus promised to the Samaritaness (John 4.14) and which flowed
from his body on the Cross (19.34). Because the river divides into
four, it becomes a symbol of the four evangelists, whose writings are
channels to us of God's loving self-revelation in Christ.

Paradisus his rigatur, part of the Sequence *Jocundare plebs fidelis*,
YM p. 203.
  This Sequence is in the style of the Victorines of Paris (see pp. 12
and 16). It was sung at St Victor and at Nevers on feasts of
Evangelists, and was added to a late thirteenth-century Sarum manu-
script (Paris, Arsenal 135) as an alternative to *Laus devota mente*. At

York it was set for the feast of St Luke; the other Evangelists were given a different Victorine-style Sequence, *Plausu chorus laetabundo*, translated in modern hymn-books as 'Come sing, ye choirs exultant'. Like the earlier part of *Jocundare* (not translated here), *Plausu chorus* applies to the Evangelists the imagery of the four creatures in Ezekiel 10.14 and Revelation 4.7.

Feasts of Martyrs

Held in Christ's hands

You are the great King's martyr
and his brave soldier.

You scorned the bloody hands of your torturers,
and clung to the strong and beautiful hands of Christ.
He alone could conquer the cruel tyrant's reign.

His holy love makes his soldiers
spendthrifts with their blood;
they gladly pour out their lives in this world
so that they can gaze on him.

NOTKER (see pp. 24–25) tries in this poem to enter imaginatively into the sufferings of a martyr as he faces death at the hands of his persecutors. As if looking through the eyes of the martyr himself, he focuses on the cruel, bloodstained hands of the men inflicting the violence. The martyr is sustained through his ordeal by an act of imaginative faith: instead of the rough hands of his tormentors, he sees in his mind the strong and beautiful hands of Christ. Those hands had known the agonizing pain of being nailed to the Cross, and it is to them that he clings in trust and love, confident that they are holding him safely and will carry him through his final agony.

In our sufferings too we can cling to those same hands, which are always there to hold and support us. While we are on earth they are hidden hands, which never diminish our freedom, but rather help us to become fully ourselves. At last, however, we shall fall into them, and only then shall we truly know how tenderly they have cherished us.

Selected verses from *Laurenti David*, Notker's Sequence for the feast of the martyred St Lawrence, NP p. 62.

This Sequence was widespread in Germany, and there are four surviving witnesses to it from England: a St Alban's manuscript of *c.* 1140, two thirteenth-century Sarum manuscripts from Exeter and London, and a Gradual of *c.* 1300 from the Augustinian house at Ranton in Staffordshire. Most places in England preferred the French Sequence for St Lawrence, *Stola jucunditatis*.

Laurenti David's melody, called *Romana*, was known all over Europe and was used for the Easter Sequence *Alleluia dic nobis* (see above, pp. 77).

Feasts of Pastors

A shepherd of souls

The welcome light of this new day has come;
a day of joy, devoted to the praise
of Christ our Saviour, who has lifted up
his holy one, and crowned him in the heavens.

The Eternal Shepherd gave to us this saint
to be a faithful shepherd of our souls;
with kindly wisdom shown in word and deed
he led the flock entrusted to his care.

The talents which God gave him multiplied
because he gave so freely of himself,
and through the faith which shone in all his life
he brought his people God's redeeming love.

With signs and wonders Christ adorned his life,
and gave his faithful servant heaven's reward;
now may his love bring healing for our wounds,
and from the darts of evil be our guard.

In John 10.11 Jesus says 'The good shepherd lays down his life for his sheep.' Christ the Good Shepherd is the model for all Christian pastors, who are called to spend themselves in caring for their flock. In thus 'losing' themselves they find their true selves. This poet sees the faithful pastor as exemplifying the teaching of the parable of the talents in Matthew 25.14ff: gifts which are put generously to use in the service of others do not become diminished by being given away, but multiply and grow richer still.

Ecce venit lux, a Sequence for confessor Bishops from a missal printed for the Francicans of Paris in 1520 (see p. 31), LS p. 329.

Feasts of Teachers

The fragrance of wisdom

He is loved by God and dear to humankind,
and his appearance is like that of an angel.
The word of life is upon his tongue,
and whoever loves him shall be blessed.

Around his mouth are courage,
knowledge, and wisdom;
his lips are choice myrrh,
distilling a fragrance of sweetness.
His body is like a finely-wrought shield
bedecked with jewels.

His way is the way of simplicity,
bringing freedom to the oppressed.
In his faith and gentleness
the Lord Almighty made him holy;
whoever holds fast to his word of wisdom
possesses the hope of life everlasting.

This fifteenth-century poet celebrates the wisdom of the saints by
drawing on the eulogy of Moses from the praises of famous men in
Ecclesiasticus (Sirach) 45.1, and he borrows a phrase from the praises
of wisdom earlier in the book at 24.15, where Wisdom says 'I have
breathed out a scent like choice myrrh'. There is also an allusion to
the wisdom found on Stephen's lips in Acts 6.15: those who heard
him 'saw that his face was like the face of an angel'.

The poem reminds us that God inspires teachers in every age to
enrich His people's lives with their wisdom, and to nourish in them
the hope of eternal life.

Dilectus Deo, a Sequence for Confessors found in several German
printed missals from the late fifteenth and early sixteenth centuries,
and in the 'Codex Brander', a sumptuous manuscript of Sequences
made at St Gall in 1507, LS p. 326.

The verse *Dilectus Deo* was the beginning of the reading
(Ecclesiasticus 45. 1–6) used as the 'Epistle' in the Mass for an Abbot.

Feasts of Women Saints

Gazing into the sun

O Church, your eyes are like sapphires
and your ears like the mount of Bethel;
your nose is a hill of myrrh and incense
and your mouth like the second of many waters.

Truly faithful to her vision,
this woman loved the Son of God;
she left behind the love of this world,
and she gazed into the sun.

She called to that most beautiful young man, saying:
'With great desire I have longed to come to you,
and to sit beside you at the heavenly marriage-feast;
rushing towards you along a strange and unknown path,
like a cloud rushing across a sky of clearest sapphire-blue.'

HILDEGARD OF BINGEN (see p. 88) wrote this Sequence for the nuns of her Rhineland convent to sing on the feast of St Ursula. She uses bridal imagery from the Song of Songs in her own distinctively creative way to portray the saint's love and longing for Christ. In Hildegard's imagination the saint as an individual becomes identified with the symbolic figure of the Church as the Bride of Christ. Her poetry is like a changing kaleidoscope full of vivid images: the sapphire of the bride's eyes is transformed into the blue of the sky, where the wind-blown cloud is carried swiftly along its high, unknown path. So, too, the saint follows her own strange and unknown path, which will lead her to her beloved Lord.

Selected verses from *O Ecclesia*, Hildegard's Sequence for the feast of St Ursula and the Eleven Thousand Virgins, AH p. 490.

This feast originated in the veneration of some nameless virgin martyrs at Cologne. In a ninth-century sermon their deaths were attributed to the persecution of Maximian. According to later medieval legend their leader Ursula was a British princess who took eleven thousand virgins with her on pilgrimage to Rome. As they were returning home, she and her companions were massacred by the Huns at Cologne. The legend gained credence in the twelfth century through the discovery, in 1106, of a burial ground near the church of St Ursula in Cologne, which was interpreted as being the resting-place of these women.

Feasts of the Blessed Virgin Mary

See '25 March', *The lion and the lamb*, p. 155 or '15 August', *A woman clothed with the sun* p. 165.

Feasts of English Saints

Bearers of the light

The Rising Sun of Justice
has graciously shone upon all the ends of the earth
through the servants who bear his light.

Praise to him
who gave this saint to the English people,
to be a lantern of his salvation,
a good teacher,
and one who helps them by his prayers.

This antiphon was written for the feast of St Cuthbert about the year 930 in the Kingdom of Wessex (see p. 63). At that time Athelstan's kingdom was a lonely outpost of Christian learning and culture in the midst of a land which had been devastated by the incursions of the Vikings. For this author, however, no situation is beyond the reach of God's redeeming love. The light of Christ, the Sun of Justice, shines to the furthest ends of the world, and his saints are like lanterns, aflame with the love of God, who carry the light of that love into the darkness of human lives. The effect of their ministry is not confined to their earthly life-times: their work lives on in all who follow their teachings, and through the Communion of Saints they continue to exercise their kindly influence by their unseen fellowship in love and prayer.

Oriens sol, an Antiphon to the *Magnificat* from Vespers of St Cuthbert, RC p. 170.

This Wessex manuscript consists of Bede's two *Lives of Cuthbert*, together with a liturgical supplement from which this antiphon comes. King Athelstan presented the manuscript to Cuthbert's shrine at Durham.

Part III

Pastoral Occasions

Mothering Sunday

see 'Fourth Sunday of Lent', *The cost of motherhood: Mary at the Cross*, p. 61.

Dedication Festival:

Sharing the worship of heaven, p. 133, or *The spiritual marriage*, p. 50.

Harvest Festival

Praise from all Creation

All the world's creatures praise You, O God;
the sun and moon and all that You have made in the heavens
     worship You,
blending their voices with the deep and mighty rivers.

The fruitful earth sings to You,
all the bright stars rejoice before You,
each living being which You have redeemed adores You and
     loves You.

Let our hearts too proclaim Your praise,
since You have filled us all with Your gracious gifts.

Possess our souls and bodies now, O Christ,
and bring us to that lovely dwelling-place on high,
where light eternal flows from Your bright glory.

God's non-human creatures glorify Him simply by being themselves. As rational beings, part of our vocation is to give explicit expression to their wordless worship and their delight in His gift of life. The gracious gifts with which God fills us at Harvest-time are tokens of His love. They point beyond themselves to a still greater gift which He longs to give us: the gift of Himself. Responding thankfully to these gifts involves an increased delight in and care for this precious fragile earth, and a greater resolve to share its resources more justly.

O Deus omnis from *Resonet sacrata*, SM p. 471.
     This eleventh-century Pentecost Sequence probably originates from Aquitaine. It was widely sung in France and England, being set in the

thirteenth-century Sarum Use for Whit Monday. Its melody, called *Paratum cor*, is given in Anselm Hughes, *Anglo-French Sequelae*, p. 62.

Although Harvest Festivals have the feel of belonging to an immemorial tradition of folk religion, they are in fact a Victorian invention. They were apparently started by the famously eccentric Parson Hawker of Morwenstow in Cornwall. (He had each of the chimneys of his vicarage built to illustrate a different architectural style, but preferred to work in a little wooden hut on the cliffs, smoking his Latakia tobacco!) In the Middle Ages, however, there were various occasions when God was publicly thanked in church for the fruits of the earth, and His blessing was asked upon them. The name 'Lammas' for the feast of St Peter's Chains on 1 August derives from 'Loaf Mass', when a loaf made from the first-ripe corn was blessed on the altar. Eggs and dairy produce were blessed at Easter, and apples on St James' Day.

Baptism

The water of life

At the very beginning of the world
Your Spirit, O God, brooded over the waters,
and thus the element of water
received its power to sanctify.

We ask You, O Lord,
to look upon the face of Your Church,
and to multiply in her Your acts of new creation.

The flowing river of Your grace
gives joy to Your city,
and You open the fountain of baptism to the whole world
for the renewal of the nations,
so that, by Your royal power,
Your people may receive through the Holy Spirit
the grace of Your beloved Son.

The author of this prayer alludes to the beginning of the Creation story, where 'the Spirit of God moved over the face of the waters' (Genesis 1.2). Water appears many times in the Bible as an image of the life-giving activity of God's Spirit, which brings joy and fertile growth. The prayer quotes one such passage from the Psalms: 'The rivers of the flood thereof make glad the city of God' (Psalm 46.4). In Baptism this poetic image becomes a sacramental reality: in and through its waters the new life of Christ is poured out, nourishing in those who receive it the seeds of potential growth as yet unseen, but full of promise for the future. Each new-born child of God has a unique place in His family, and the stream of grace which springs from the font will go on flowing until all the baptized reach the full stature of their completed growth in Christ.

Deus cuius spiritus, part of the Blessing of the Font on Holy Saturday, which was the traditional time for Baptism in the early Church, SM p. 128.

Confirmation

The life-giving Spirit

You proceed, O Comforter,
from the Father and the Son:
give us tongues to speak Your praise,
set our minds and hearts ablaze
with Your flame, O Holy One.

All things live and move in You,
loving warmth of sanctity:
bond of love that joins in one
God the Father and the Son,
equal in divinity.

Shining light of love divine,
bring our darkened hearts release:
chase the shadows which we dread,
guide our steps, that we may tread
paths of justice and of peace.

Fears and worries melt away
in the warmth of Your blest fire:
may the joyful love You bring
lead to our true flourishing
and fulfil our hearts' desire.

Confirmation sets the seal on the process of initiation into the Church and is a means of grace to meet the challenges of mature Christian living. The Holy Spirit, the bond of love between the Persons of the Trinity, is given to the members of Christ's Body the Church to help them grow in their love for God and one another, so that they may embody God's love in the world.

Selected verses from *Qui procedis*, a Victorine Sequence (see pp. 12 and 16) for Pentecost dating from the twelfth century, LS p. 112.

Adam of St Victor is now thought not to have been Adam Brito (d. 1192) but another Adam who entered St Victor after having been Precentor of Notre Dame and who died in 1146. Margot Fassler [in *Gothic Song* (Cambridge 1993), pp. 277–8] thinks that *Qui procedis* dates from the generation after Adam: its Trinitarian theology, especially the idea that the love between Christians should reflect the love between the Persons of the Trinity, is reminiscent of Richard of St Victor's *De Trinitate*. (Richard died in 1173.)

Qui procedis was sung at St Victor and Notre Dame but its use seems to have been confined to the city of Paris, not even reaching as far as St Denis. It did, however, survive in the Parisian repertoire into the sixteenth century, since it is commented on by Clichtoveus in his *Elucidarium* of 1517.

First Communion:

see 'Proper 15, Year B', *The joy of Christ's presence*, p. 122.

Blessing of a marriage

A prayer for guidance in the way of love

May God send to you His holy angel from His heavenly throne
to strengthen you in your service of Him,
to show you the way of justice,
and to defend you always from every evil.

God willed that His only Son, our Lord Jesus Christ,
should be born into this world as its Redeemer;
he consecrated the marriage at Cana by his presence and first
    miracle
when he changed the water into wine;
may he also be present at your marriage to sanctify it and bless it.

May he grant you peaceful times and health of mind and body.
When the labours of this life are over,
may he lead you into the happy fellowship of the holy angels.

May God, whose kingdom and power are everlasting, grant you
    this blessing,
and may His peace be with you for ever.

Austin Farrer said in a wedding sermon 'It is not surprising ... that
Christ should begin his ministry at a wedding: for a true marriage is
a special favour of God's grace, and a direct foretaste of heaven.
God's glory is reflected, for those who truly love, in one another's
faces; they see the Creator shining through his handiwork, and the
vision inspires them with a simple delight in doing one another good,
and in furthering God's will. Those who are being married ... do not,
as the rest of us so often must, make themselves care about the will of
God: they do care for it: for they care for one another.'

Ipse a supernis, a Marriage Blessing from the Benedictional of
Archbishop Robert (see p. 20), BR p. 151.
    This prayer is a later addition to the manuscript made in the
Province of Rouen about the year 1200.
    The quotation from Austin Farrer comes from a wedding sermon
preached in 1966 and published in *A Celebration of Faith* (London
1970), pp. 136–7.

Communion of the sick:

see 'Proper 13, Year B', *Bread of life*, p. 119.

A prayer with someone who is ill

Held within the love of the Trinity

May you be blessed by God the Father,
who created all things from the beginning.

May you be blessed by God the Son,
who came down from his throne on high for our salvation,
and consented to suffer on the cross.

May you be blessed by the Holy Spirit,
who, in the likeness of a dove,
rested upon Christ in the River Jordan.

May God the Holy Trinity
watch over your body
and preserve your soul.

May He shine within your heart
and guide your thoughts.
May His grace increase and flourish within you.
May He set you free from all evil
and wipe out all your sins.
May His right hand protect you,
and lead you to the life of heaven.

In sickness and in health we are unfailingly held within the love of the Trinity. The Cross reveals that our God is not a distant potentate, but a Father who is irrevocably bound to us in love, and who suffers in all our suffering. The Spirit of Life, which fills His eternal Son, lives and breathes in us too.

An abbreviated version of *Benedicat te*, the long blessing which formed the conclusion to the Sarum Order for the Visitation of the Sick, SM p. 423.

This Order consisted of the Lord's Prayer, some versicles and responses, and a series of short prayers, followed by Confession, Anointing, and Communion. At the beginning of the rite is the rubric 'On the way, let them say the seven penitential psalms'. This assumes that other people would be with the priest when he made his visit.

Pastoral visits can bear unexpected fruit: it was this piece of domestic liturgy that was the occasion of Julian of Norwich's 'Revelations of Divine Love'. Her account of these 'showings' is now recognized as a spiritual classic. On 8 May 1373 Julian was apparently nearing the end of what was thought to be her last illness, and her parish priest was sent for. As directed by the *Sarum Manual*, before beginning the rite of Visitation he held up a crucifix for Julian to look at. Julian describes what happened next: 'He set the cross before my face and said, "I have brought you the image of your Maker and Saviour. Look at it, and be strengthened." ... Then my sight began to fail, and the room became dark about me, as if it were night, except for the image of the cross which somehow was lighted up; ... Suddenly all my pain was taken away, and I was as fit and well as I had ever been; ... And at once I saw the red blood trickling down from under the garland; ... At the same moment the Trinity filled me full of heartfelt joy.' [*Revelations of Divine Love*, ed. C. Wolters (Harmondsworth 1966), pp. 65–6.]

For the dead:

see 'All Souls' Day', *Cherishing those who have died*, p. 171.

A prayer with the bereaved

Entrusting our loved one to God

Our hearts are wounded and stricken
with the shock of grief.
In the midst of our sorrow
we turn to you, Redeemer of the world.

As the soul of our loved one now comes to you,
the fountain of goodness,
we ask you to receive it in your mercy
with your sweet gentleness.

Whatever faults and imperfections it had while on earth,
take them away, O Lord,
and forget them for ever.

Grant that our loved one may be joined
to the company of your saints at the Resurrection.

This prayer does not attempt to gloss over the shock and hurt of
bereavement with pious platitudes. Grief is a wound which takes time
to heal. There is no suggestion that Christian people ought not to feel
sorrow when someone they love dies. The sorrow is recognized as
natural and inevitable, but in the midst of it we can turn to Christ, the
Redeemer of the world. He shares our humanity and knows what it is
to suffer and to grieve. He is the conqueror of death and the fountain
of mercy; we can commend our loved one with confidence into his
gentle hands.

Diri vulneris, SM p. 429.
    This prayer formed part of the Sarum office for the Commendation
of a Soul.

Before a pilgrimage or journey

Christ our companion on the way

May Almighty God graciously direct you on your journey,
and bring you in safety
to the place where you wish to go,
for His merciful love is known in all places,
and He treats His family with tender kindness.

May a band of angels go with you
and prepare the way before you;
may their comfort sustain you
and protect your path from harm.

May Christ who is the Way, the Truth, and the Life
be your companion;
may you follow the way of justice
and reach the reward of everlasting joy.

Many religious traditions use the idea of a journey as a metaphor of life itself. The making of a pilgrimage concentrates into a microcosm many aspects of our lives of which most of the time we are only subliminally aware. For example, whether we like it or not, we are surrounded each day by a good deal of uncertainty. Staying at home can easily blind us to this fact, but going on a journey makes us face up to it. If we are to grow healthily, we must accept the often uncomfortable truth that life inevitably involves flux and change, that 'here we have no continuing city' (Hebrews 13.14). The alternative is an escape into sterile fantasy, a clinging to idols which need to be outgrown. The one reliable constant is God Himself: He is not only the goal of our pilgrimage, He is also with us at every step of our way. The uncertainty which is built into the world's fabric is the tool of His providential care, and our security lies in putting our hand into His.

Omnipotens Deus, a blessing for those about to set out on a pilgrimage or journey, from the Benedictional of Archbishop Robert (see p. 20), BR p. 55.

A prayer in anxiety:

see 'Proper 4, Year A', *Founded on God's peace*, p. 97.

For the guidance of the Holy Spirit:

see 'Fourth Sunday before Lent, Year A', *A prayer for God's grace*, p. 40.

Christian Unity:

see 'Proper 11, Year C', *Mutual love and peace*, p. 114.

For the peace of the world:

see 'Proper 9, Year C', *Christ our peace*, p. 112.

Before a Bible Study:

see 'Proper 25, Option B – Bible Sunday', *A prayer for deeper under-standing*, p. 132.

The Blessed Sacrament:

see 'Corpus Christi', *The banquet of delight*, p. 95;
or 'Proper 12, Year B', *Bread from heaven*, p. 117;
or 'Proper 13, Year B', *Bread of life*, p. 119;
or 'Proper 14, Year B', *Foretaste of heaven*, p. 121;
or 'Proper 15, Year B', *The joy of Christ's presence* p. 122.

The Sacred Heart:

see 'Third Sunday of Lent', *The stream of love*, p. 59.

The Blessed Virgin Mary:

see '25 March', *The lion and the lamb*, p. 155;
or '15 August', *A woman clothed with the sun*, p. 165.

Our Lady of Sorrows:

see 'Fourth Sunday of Lent', *The cost of motherhood: Mary at the Cross*, p.61;
or 'Good Friday', *Mary's grief*, p. 71.

Stewardship Renewal

Bound together by Christ's love

The love of Christ has gathered us in one:
let us rejoice and all be glad in him;
let us revere and love the living God
and love each other truly from our hearts.
Where charity and love are, there is God.

Love is the highest good, the fullest gift;
all precepts and commandments hang on love,
and love is the fulfilling of the law;
it carries those it fills to highest heaven.
Where charity and love are, there is God.

Let us then love God with all our heart,
preferring nothing to our love for Him,
and love our neighbours as we love ourselves,
and even enemies, for Christ's dear sake.
Where charity and love are, there is God.

Those who keep this two-fold rule of love
and try to follow it with humble mind,
they truly live in Christ; Christ lives in them,
and drives away sin's darkness from their hearts.
Where charity and love are, there is God.

PAULINUS OF AQUILEIA (*c.* 730–802) wrote this Hymn to Love for a synod at Friuli in 796. Conflict and controversy are inevitably part of the life of the Church in every age, and doubtless the Synod of Friuli was no exception. Paulinus therefore reminds its members of the love which is at the heart of Christianity. He also sees that loving ourselves (because God loves us) goes hand in hand with loving God and other people.

The 'nuts and bolts' of church life need to be attended to, whether these are matters of worship and doctrine, or the business of making sure the church building has a watertight roof. Sometimes the detail threatens to overwhelm us, and it is at those times that Paulinus' message can be a timely reminder to us of what is at the heart of our life as members of Christ's Church. The point of all the detailed activity is simply that God's people may grow in love.

Paulinus sees that God is the source and ground of all love: every

Christian community is gathered together by the love of God in Christ, and so the process of growth in love is one in which God always takes the initiative. Part of our response to that initiative is to ask ourselves what proportion of our time, talents, and money we can give to the work of the Church, as a sign of our gratitude for all the love which God lavishes on us day by day. As St John says (1 John 4.19), 'We love, because he first loved us.'

Congregavit nos, OB p. 102.

Paulinus was a grammarian from Italy and a leading figure in that revival of European learning known as the Carolingian Renaissance. In 776 Charlemagne summoned him to join the circle of scholars at his court at Aachen, and he taught with Alcuin of York in the Palace School. In 787 he returned to his home territory on being made Patriarch of Aquileia. As a prominent churchman he necessarily became involved in the controversies of the time: he tried to promote good relations with the Eastern Church, in which the legitimacy of icons was being bitterly contested, and he wrote against the Spanish Adoptianists, who denied that Jesus was the eternal Son of God.

The monk Walafrid Strabo, writing in the 820s, tells us that Paulinus composed hymns to be sung at Mass (*De Rebus Ecclesiasticis* xxv in Migne, *Patrologia Latina*, Vol. 114, col. 954). This was worthy of note because in those days hymns were usually confined to the Offices. Parts of *Congregavit nos* are often sung at the ceremony of the Washing of Feet on Maundy Thursday, and the modern Taizé chant *Ubi caritas et amor* uses its Latin refrain.

Before a synod or meeting

The Spirit of justice and love

We are here, O Holy Spirit;
we are here, burdened by our ever-present sins,
but gathered especially in Your name.

Come to us; be present with us;
enter into our hearts with Your gentleness and grace.

Teach us what we should do;
show us where You are leading us,
and how we should go about our work.

May You alone be the prompter of our thoughts,
and our fellow-worker as we reach our decisions and put them
    into effect,
for Your name alone is glorious with God the Father and His
    Son.

Do not allow us to work against Your justice,
for You love justice above all things.

Grant us the good gifts which we ask of You;
may we make our judgements with care and wisdom,
and always be lovers of mercy;
so may our actions shine brightly before You,
and be pleasing in Your sight.

Asking God to inspire our actions does not make them any less our own. In seeking His guidance we are trying to align our wills with His. As Austin Farrer wrote, 'The control of our Creator is not an alien control, preventing us from being ourselves. The more he directs us, the more we are what we have it in us to be.'

Adsumus, a prayer before a Provincial Synod from the Benedictional of Archbishop Robert (see p. 20), BR p. 152.

Like the marriage-blessing on p. 192, this prayer is among the material added to the manuscript in the Province of Rouen about the year 1200.

The quotation from Austin Farrer comes from his Commentary on *The Revelation of St John the Divine* (Oxford 1964), p. 26.

At a Young People's Service

Stormy waters: the adventures of a swan

NARRATOR: I shall sound the lament, my sons,
                        of the winged swan who flew across the seas.
                Oh how bitterly did she bewail her fate,
                that she had left the flowery land
                and sought the ocean deeps, saying:

SWAN: Poor wretched bird that I am!
                Alas, what shall I do?
                The light has gone,
                my wings will support me no longer here in these
                        waters.
                The waves strike me,
                and storms buffet me this way and that, exiled and
                        alone.

                I am crushed between the wave-crests of the
                        swirling deep.
                I groan as I fly, unable to mount to the heavens;
                everywhere I look, death surrounds me.
                Though I can see food in plenty for fishes to eat,
                the mighty crowding waves prevent me from
                        taking it;
                I can find no good food for myself.

                East and West, all regions of the sky,
                bright and shining stars, come to assist me!
                Beg Orion that he would pursue
                and hunt the flying storm-clouds to their death.

NARRATOR: As she thought in silence on these things,
                the radiant dawn came to her aid.
                The warm breath of the day revived her,
                and she began to renew her strength.
                Jubilant, she soon climbed back to her accustomed
                        heights,
                among the clouds and the stars.
                Rejoicing greatly, with overflowing happiness,
                she crossed the ocean waters.
                Sweetly singing, she flew to the lands of delight.

> All you hosts of winged creatures, come and
> proclaim:

CHORUS: To the great King be glory!

This ninth-century mystical poem could be performed simply as a dramatic reading, or (depending on the available resources, both human and electrical!) with the addition of mime, dance, lighting effects, and music. 'Stormy' music could subside into a short silence before the narrator's second speech, and then the coming of dawn could be portrayed by gradually increasing light, and quiet pastoral music which builds to a climax for the final chorus of praise.

Clangam filii, OB p. 90.

The poem was used as a Sequence for ordinary Sundays at Limoges and Winchester in the tenth century. In the earliest of the Aquitanian tropers (Paris, BN lat. 1240, from St Martial, Limoges, *c.* 930) it is interpreted as an allegory of the Fall (the swan's leaving the flowery land) and Redemption (the 'dawn from on high' which saves her). Orion the Hunter is the constellation which dominates the southern sky in winter. His hunting-dog Sirius, the fiercely-shining Dog Star, follows at his heels.

The melody of *Clangam* (or, in some manuscripts, *Plangant*) *filii* is called *Planctus cygni*, the 'Swan's Lament'. It is given by Anselm Hughes in *Anglo-French Sequelae* on p. 63. *Olim lacus*, the Swan's Lament in the twelfth-century *Carmina Burana* from Benediktbeuern in Germany, may possibly be a parody of *Clangam*. The German swan is being roasted and eaten! *Clangam* did not survive after the twelfth century; its last appearance is in BL Roy. 8 C xiii, a Norman manuscript dating from *c.* 1100.